On the Land of My Father

T0276994

On the Land of My Father

A Farm Upbringing in Segregated Mississippi

BEVELYN CHARLENE EXPOSÉ

McFarland & Company, Inc., Publishers

Jefferson, North Carolina

LIBRARY OF CONGRESS CATALOGUING-IN-PUBLICATION DATA

Exposé, Bevelyn Charlene, 1939–
    On the land of my father : a farm upbringing in segregated
Mississippi / Bevelyn Charlene Exposé.
        p.   cm.
    Includes index.

    ISBN 978-0-7864-7850-7 (softcover : alk. paper) ∞
    ISBN 978-1-4766-1352-9 (ebook)

    1. Exposé, Bevelyn Charlene, 1939– —Childhood and youth.
2. African American women—Mississippi—Sumrall—Biography.
3. African Americans—Mississippi—Sumrall—Biography.
4. African Americans—Mississippi—Sumrall—Social life and
customs—20th century.   5. Sumrall (Miss.)—Social life and
customs—20th century.   6. Exposé, Bevelyn Charlene, 1939–
—Family.   7. Farm life—Mississippi—Sumrall.   8. Sumrall
(Miss.)—Race relations.   I. Title.

F349.S95E97 2014
976.2'19063092—dc23
    [B]   2014000848

BRITISH LIBRARY CATALOGUING DATA ARE AVAILABLE

On the cover: the author at the age of three, 1942; other images ©
Thinkstock

Manufactured in the United States of America

McFarland & Company, Inc., Publishers
  Box 611, Jefferson, North Carolina 28640
    www.mcfarlandpub.com

In memory of my parents,
Noah Henry and Etta Mae Dukes Exposé,
and my sister, Darlene Exposé Diggs

Acknowledgments

Many thanks to:

Diane
Gayle
Katrina
Lynda
Mona
Nikki
Yolonda

Contents

*The lives of the dead are centered
in the memories of the living.* — Cicero

Preface

This is a story that takes place in the middle of the twentieth century, in the segregated Deep South of Mississippi. It was a time in history when the Negro was not always considered fully human and generally nothing more than a good field hand. It's a story that's part of the American past few readers have read much about. It's a story of work, family and community that is bittersweet because it no longer exists. It is a lived history of country life on my father's farm and the story of black farmers' gifts to their country. It is a narrative that has been seriously omitted from the repertory of most publishers and one that needs to be remembered and handed down.

I was born October 4, 1939, to a black landowning family in rural Mississippi, the twelfth of thirteen children. My father was Noah Henry Exposé (May 24, 1893–February 21, 1983) and my mother was Etta Mae Dukes Exposé (December 3, 1898–February 1, 1976). My brothers and sisters were: Noah Jr. (September 25, 1918–May 17, 2002), Luther (March 14, 1921–January 7, 2010), Clifford (June 27, 1923–May 2, 1988), Bufford (August 8, 1925–July 20, 1998), Loretta (October 8, 1927–December 7, 1993), Daniel (March 13, 1932–December 20, 1980), Myrtis (April 12, 1936–September 25, 2001), twins Celestine ("Jimmy") (August 30, 1938–February 23, 1964) and Earldeen (August 30, 1938–December 21, 1938), and Darlene (July 6, 1942–September 8, 2013). My living siblings are Carzella, born March 10, 1930; and Paul, born March 27, 1934.

I believe the kind of person you become is based on the principles of life you are taught through the examples of the people around you and from the groundwork laid by your parents. By the time I was six or seven years old, a sense of right and wrong, fair play, belief in myself and lack of fear had begun to form the person I am today. My Mississippi childhood was my greatest inheritance.

My readings over the years in libraries and book stores about southern Negro farm life has led me to write about my family from a different perspective. Some of my readings, such as *The Bottom Rung*, a study of southern black farmers, focuses on women and children. It portrays southern farm women as the glue that held families together as they worked alongside their husbands in the fields. The book states that in 1994 black lawyers outnumbered black farmers 10 to 1, that there were only 2,906 black farm operators or managers in the United States, about 0.02 percent of the entire employed African American civilian labor force. That book, like mine, ascribes great value to the labor of black women farmers and their power both within the family and in the community. While it indicates that children contributed much to farm work, my book shows the history behind that work and the long, rich legacy of family values derived from it. In it, Stewart Tolnay focuses on the present; I show the importance of the past, which can illuminate all that is missing in our culture today—for example, pride in one's labor, respect for elders as a source of wisdom and authority, a sense of responsibility to one's community and society. While I acknowledge the urban black statesmen in my own family, I also show that land ownership gave us a reason to invest in farming and commit to it as a way of life.

Another book, *Trouble in Mind*, draws on first-person narratives and a variety of artifacts from both blacks and whites. Leon Litwack shows how black southerners strived for education in a system that imposed separate and unequal opportunities. At the end of the nineteenth and beginning of the twentieth centuries, tenant farmers were cheated and dispossessed, ambitious blacks were targeted with violence, and all were subjected to white oppression. A manipulated judi-

Noah Exposé driving a tractor in his cotton field in 1950.

cial system and enforced ignorance led to poverty and misery, but some black families found refuge in their own religion, work, music, and humor.

Like Litwack, I also draw on first-person tales. Mine have been passed down to me by spoken words. I describe in detail the artifacts and rituals that made up our daily life. While I allude to the hypocrisies and contradictions that failed my people in the same time period that Litwack addresses, I move beyond that to show the triumphs of perseverance and protest. My book focuses on the affirmative aspects of our lives, because violence and misery were not the predominant forces

3

of the southern Mississippi farming life I knew. My family lived in prosperity, due to faith, discipline, hard work, and contributions to the community.

Another reading, *Homecoming*, illustrates the history of African American farmers. The book is based on the film *Homecoming* and is a companion book to that documentary. It traces black land ownership from the Reconstruction era to the recent Supreme Court decision to compensate black farmers for racist banking practices. Based on personal memory, it is a requiem for a past way of life.

My book also offers images of Mississippi farm life in the middle of the last century and traces the history of a land-owning family of black farmers, but this history begins long before the Reconstruction era. While my pages are filled with personal memory, they provide well researched information as well — documents of the accomplishments of my immediate and extended families. The tone is not that of a requiem but of celebration, an appreciation of all that land ownership gave us, which allowed us to become full and avid citizens with a contribution to make to society. My book explains why our family was able to withstand the hardships and challenges of farming and why I am happy to return to the place where I was born.

Me in 2013.

Another of my readings, *Mama Learned Us to Work: Farm Women in the New South*, uses oral histories as source material. Lu Ann Jones shows how southern farm women bargained with

4

peddlers as consumers and developed the "butter and egg trade" as producers, which offered a cushion of economic support during the 1920s and 1930s and independence from their menfolk. They laid the foundation for the poultry agribusiness that followed World War II. Both black and white home demonstration agents helped link their clients to government resources.

While I feature beautiful portraits of my mother and her sisters and my grandmothers and great-grandmothers as women of initiative, enterprise, and success in their farming ventures, I also show them as working side by side with the men. Never inferior or secondary to their male counterparts, they also never stopped working. Yet, it was not only the women who performed multiple jobs (farming, cooking, housekeeping, child care, church and school service) but also the men. My father farmed but also did carpentry and masonry; his brothers also worked as clergy. My book shows that because of their multifaceted skills and efforts, women were never less than the backbone of the community. I show several instances when they display the ability to run a farm and raise a family by themselves; but the women of my family did not need to because of the respect they commanded from their husbands and the faith that held the family together.

My story is not about:

- The self-contempt that results in the social dysfunction of the working poor;
- Guilt, deceit, and "passing over" from black or native to white society by changing names, hiding family relations, inventing a background or creating a new past;
- Hostility toward white America.

Through the wide array of tales I re-create and pass on, *On the Land of My Father* calls attention to the legacies of black, native and white southerners as the fascination they were for each other, all the while sharing a common relationship to the land. I challenge the simplistic notion that a life of picking cotton in the state most emblematic

GREAT-GRANDPARENTS

Elias Exposé
- Stephen
- Harry
- Ocia
- Mary
- Daniel
- Willis
- Paul
- Emma - Silas

Margaret Exposé

Hardy Lee
- Eran
- Joe
- Mary

Alice Lee

Anderson Dukes
- Julia
- Allen
- Emanuel
- Gabriel
- Gilbert
- Mary
- John

Viney Dukes

Gustave Jefferson
- Sarah
- Sophronia
- Albert
- Polly
- Josh
- Hannah

Irene Jefferson

GRANDPARENTS

Daniel Exposé
- Luther
- Noah Henry
- Byron

Eran Lee Exposé

Emanuel Dukes
- Sarah
- Gilbert
- Maud
- Julia
- Artis
- Montes
- Roxanna
- Etta Mae
- Gladys

Sophronia Jefferson Dukes

PARENTS

Noah Henry Exposé
- Noah Jr.
- Luther
- Clifford
- Bufford
- Loretta
- Carzella
- Daniel Emanuel
- Paul Evans
- Myrtis Easter
- Earldene & Celestine (Twins)
- Bevelyn Charlene
- Darlene

Etta Mae Dukes Exposé

Bevelyn Charlene

of the crop meant only pain and hostility, because in my direct experience the values and aspirations derived from such labor bonded us to each other in spite of the fact that the civil rights fought for in my era and earlier have still not been adequately enforced by law to this day. In *On the Land of My Father: A Farm Upbringing,* I will take you on a journey begun by a man called Noah, a name out of the Bible. His parents were all about religion, education, and family, a combination that created a force in him that kept his mind, spirit and innate need to succeed intact.

As I reflect on my early years, I can still feel the sweat running down my face and the stretch of my back as I drew my body upright to work in the fields. I was a skinny little girl, and now I walk tall with the riches of my family. Not everyone today can look back on their childhood labor and discipline as a gift. If you have never experienced working on the land, you have never really known it nor grown with its seasons of toil and harvest. My family's fortune was its debt to the land, a resource that endowed us with incredible responsibility and the inspiration to fulfill it. There on that Mississippi farm were food and friends and family that sustained me, the land giving back what we put into it and more.

Chapter 1

On Papa's Farm, in Mama's Kitchen

Papa's Farm

The Color Line Moves with the Horizon

My first memory of a cotton field was as a four-year-old in the 1940s, riding on the tail end of Papa's old mule-drawn wagon, my dangling legs flopping about on our way up to the cotton field. Old Emma, our favorite mule, was too old to plow, but she was strong and sturdy enough to pull the wagon for a short distance — all without stopping to rest, drink water, or eat hay.

It was already hot out and not yet ten o'clock in the morning. An old pickup truck came roaring down the gravel road, stirring up more dust than a windstorm. My big straw hat kept the sun off my face but couldn't keep the dust out of my eyes. Grabbing the hem of my dress, I spit on it and wiped my eyes. My sisters, Myrtis, seven, and Jimmy, five, sat with me. They knew how to cover their faces and turned their heads away from the cloud of dust.

One of my brothers, Dan or Paul, would take turns driving the wagon up to the field. The dust settled as we got closer, and Old Emma walked a little slower. Along the way, down the hill, on the right side of the road, grew Papa's big green bean and black-eyed pea patch —

much bigger than Mama's garden. At the foot of the hill was a cement tunnel bridge hidden by woods and fields on both sides of the road. The bridge went over a creek that ran through the woods, down to the back pasture behind the barn, and ended up by the gravel pit.

The only houses on the road before our cotton fields belonged to white people, Miss Vera and Barry, about 400 feet west of us. Barry was one of old man Walter Harris's sons and he lived 500 feet down the road east of our house. Barry and Vera had a small farm on the right and left side of the road between our fields.

The old wagon squeaked less as it turned the curve past Miss Vera's house. Coming up the road, we could see a little cotton house on the left side of the field. Being allowed to leap into the big piles of cotton was my treat for the day. Myrtis and Jimmy played in it a little, but they liked to go outside and walk between the cotton rows. Rolling around in the fluffy, soft cotton and scooping up the white puffs and tossing them over my head was my particular joy — it was like jumping on a cloud.

Cotton fields were everywhere. The two largest were 40 acres each and located on the upper road. One small field lay on the south side of our house, another on the east side. A fifth, smaller, field was across the back road where Papa and his brother, Uncle Luther, grew up and where Grandma and Grandpa lived in their old house. Because the three of us girls were not old enough to pick cotton, Mama always told us to come back to the house after we got up to the field, and we did.

Walking on the road with the little ditches and embankments on the sides was an adventure. The wind rattled the leaves on the tall trees that lined the road and I'd run down the ditch and up the embankment, singing "down in the valley, up on the mountain." Wild flowers grew along the road in summer and autumn — black-eyed Susan and white, blue, and purple morning glory everywhere. All summer, the smell of honeysuckle sweetened the air. The wind carried the scent all down the road. Jimmy and Myrtis would just walk down the road talking.

Myrtis was big for her age, tall and large-boned enough to fight. Jimmy and I were shorter and skinnier. No one ever bothered us children walking down the road. Everybody knew who we were: Mae and Noah's children.

As we got older and did little things around the house, we had specific chores—not so much because Mama told us to, but because we favored certain things. Myrtis was good at cooking and ironing with white flour starch: Papa's white shirts, Dan and Paul's Levis. Jimmy was good at sweeping the floor, playing the piano, and gathering eggs. I liked milking the cow as soon as I was big enough to hold a bucket between my knees. Darlene, the youngest, didn't do too much of anything. We picked peas, green beans, collards, turnips, mustards, sweet peas (also known as sugar peas or snow peas), beets, and tomatoes from Mama's garden as long as they lasted.

When I was about nine, Paul gave me a sack and showed me how to pick cotton along his row. He taught me to use only my fingers to pull the cotton out of the burr because the pointed ends were sharp and prickly and could cause sore, painful hands if you grabbed the whole boll. I picked Dan and Paul's row, at my own pace. By the time I was twelve, I was picking a hundred pounds a day.

We had a routine at our house every day. One of us got up early and made a fire in the stove. Before daybreak, we were all out in the fields a good hour before Mama got up to cook breakfast. The wagon was always parked out in the field as we filled our sacks with cotton. I'd pull my sack behind me or throw it over my shoulder the way Paul had shown me and take the cotton to the wagon to be weighed. Papa had a scale attached to the side of the wagon that stuck out a few feet from the back and three or four feet off the ground to accommodate the weight of the sack when it was on the scale.

The bottom of my Levis would be soaked with dew, but by the time we went back up to the house to eat breakfast, the morning sun had dried them out. Every morning during cotton-picking season, Mama would have a big pan of biscuits, eggs, bacon or sausage, figs, syrup, and rice with gravy or milk for us. After breakfast, we went back to the fields until lunchtime.

Darlene would get water for us because she was too little to pick cotton. She never hurried, no matter how much Dan told her to. By the time she got back with the water, the bucket was only half full and covered with leaves and trash because Darlene swung the bucket back and forth between the cotton rows. Each time Dan told her to go back and get more water, it'd be the same. "We can't drink that water," he would say.

Out in the field, we talked about everybody in school, church and the community. We made fun of them all — the deacons who couldn't lead a hymn worth anything, sisters in the church who wore their hats backward and stocking seams on the side of their legs, teachers who dressed in old-fashioned clothes, Dan and Paul's ugly girlfriends— nothing was left out. We talked about Jimmy's piano playing, about Myrtis's primping, and about playing basketball. We made fun of the women who shouted in church, discussed which preacher couldn't preach well, and imitated them. I talked about how I wanted to go to faraway places.

What was fun and most important to me was Paul teaching me how to fight right in the middle of the cotton field. (This was before Papa started hiring all the hired hands.) Paul showed me how to block, duck and punch, to punch as hard as I could when I hit someone. This would pay off years later. But as children, we never fought or argued with each other. Mama didn't allow it. There was no sibling rivalry. All of us had our own interests and things to do. To me, the farm was the best place to be. The open space and the clean air. Walking in the woods along the fences that separated Papa's land from the Harris's land. The feel of cool dirt under my bare feet, riding in the wagon, riding behind Dan on Old Emma, the mule. All the things I loved to eat that grew underground, like sweet potatoes and peanuts; and above the ground, like sugarcane, strawberries and watermelon; or on vines, like grapes. And all the raw vegetables in the garden. The land was the driving force behind the hard work. Everything could be planted and eaten. And so many things grew wild: blackberries, blueberries, plum trees in the woods, and a tart apple tree.

Two sisters, older than Dan and Paul, were already away from home. Carzella married when I was eight and moved to Bassfield, Mississippi, a year before I started picking cotton. Loretta left home to finish high school and go to college up at Tougaloo, outside Jackson. My older brother Bufford lived up at Grandma's and Grandpa's; Clifford, Luther (Tootsie), and Noah Jr. (Boy Noah), were all off to war when I was four. Only the last six of us grew up together. It's that way when you come from a big family. Siblings are separated into groups based on their ages.

Cotton: The Cash Crop

Cotton was the big cash crop every year and the acreage grew over the years. But there were a few other small crops, especially cucumbers and corn. Sweet potatoes, sugarcane, and white potatoes were for personal use and so were the peach orchard, the big grapevine that Papa built a scaffold around, watermelons, and Grandma's strawberries. Cotton grows in hot weather and needs fertile, well-drained soil in order to get good moisture during the growing season. The weather has to be sunny after the bolls open because it helps to dry the fibers. Nitrogen, potassium and phosphorous were in the fertilizer Papa put in the soil.

What I remember is Papa, Dan and Paul clearing the fields where Papa was going to plant cotton for that year. They loosened up the dirt by a lot of plowing and tilling so that when the seeds were dropped they were all enclosed in dirt. All the leftover trash from last year had rotted and would help fertilize the crop for the next year. Papa would plow rows of beds, which are low ridges in which to plant the seeds. He said the beds were better than a flat area because they kept the seeds at a warmer temperature but didn't keep in excess moisture.

Papa at his other "home" — the cotton field, 1950.

Papa had a seed planter, a piece of equipment like a plow with handles, which was pulled by a mule to drop the seeds. He planted a lot of seeds in each group, a little thicker than usual, so that enough seeds came up. Sometimes if enough seeds didn't come up, he said it was because too few were planted in each row, and if it rained a lot before harvesting the bolls wouldn't open properly and would become "storm damaged." If the bolls weren't clean, the money they drew was less per pound, reducing the crop to "Grade B" instead of "Grade A" cotton. Papa said that sometimes if the crop didn't come up, a farmer would have to replant his whole crop, or if he was lucky he'd only have to fill in the wide spaces where it hadn't come up.

For years, we didn't have trouble with boll weevils. But by the 1930s, Papa started to have the fields sprayed to prevent infestation.

14

There was a white man who lived a mile or so up the road and had a small plane that he used to spray farmers' crops around the whole area. By the late 1940s, Papa had two tractors and many different pieces of equipment that could be attached to the tractors that did the breaking up, tilling and cutting of the soil. A seed planter or duster was attached to the tractor with a long arm that reached high over the rows to dust the cotton. The same cotton-seed planter would be installed to plant corn seeds by Papa's simply inserting a different plate.

Papa planted cotton in early April, and it took only about a week for the seeds to come up. Once the stalk reached three or four inches high, we had to scrape the cotton with a hoe, a long handle with a thick blade across the bottom. It was flat and square and was used to separate the stalks so they could grow better without being too thick. By August, it was time to pick our cotton. I don't think Papa ever had a bad year or a bad crop, especially not a bad crop of cotton. And every year, he planted more and more.

Cucumbers: The Other Cash Crop

When I walk down the aisle in a supermarket and see all the jars of pickles lined up on the shelf, it takes me back to my childhood. It was a time when the early morning dew was still on the ground and a field job seemed like punishment to me. I wonder if most people who buy pickles really know what it takes to get them on the shelves. First, the cucumbers are planted in March; by June, they're ready to be picked. The vines grow long and thin and are tangled in all directions but are extremely fragile. They grow flat on the ground. We had to be careful where to put our feet because if we stepped on the vine, it could easily break. The leaves were wide and big and had fuzzy little hairs that stung the skin. A long-sleeved shirt was a necessity to wear, so the hands got the brunt of the sting. Every couple of days was time to pick cucumbers, because the smaller ones brought the most money at the vat.

A big machine separated the cucumbers based on size. Smaller ones were used for canning pickles that lined the shelves. Papa fed the hogs with the big ones, and Mama would slice them with tomatoes to make a salad. Sometimes Papa would let me drive the pickup truck out to the cucumber vat. It was in a little one-horse town called Sumrall, Mississippi, about eight miles east of us. I don't think it had a stoplight back then. As the cucumber fields grew, Sumrall became important to us.

Field of Gold

Corn was the other crop. Papa planted 50 acres a year in March or April, depending on the weather. He had a certain type of "plate" on a seed dropper to drop seeds about seven inches apart so they had room to grow. After the corn came up and was six to eight inches tall, it had to be thinned with a hoe just as the cotton did. We were out every day from sunup to sundown thinning corn and dropping soda fertilizer around the young stalks.

October was harvest time. Two corn houses were at the edge of the field and one was in the barnyard. They were kept full of corn until the next year's harvest. That corn fed the cows, mules, hogs and chickens all year long.

Tenant Farmer

Every year our cotton fields grew bigger, and more land was bought. All the other fields grew too—Irish potatoes, corn, cucumbers, big patches of black-eyed peas and green beans. With only my younger brothers Dan and Paul at home, Papa needed more men to help run the farm. Girls didn't plow; tenant farmers were the answer.

There were two older houses on the farm already—one up the road near the two big cotton fields that was a four-room house big enough for a man, his wife and a couple of children. The other house was bigger, with six rooms, and the last was a little, three-room house at the edge of our yard that Papa built for a man and wife. Most houses back then had small rooms, and the kitchen, eating area and living area were all one big room centered by a fireplace. There were no closets or indoor toilets. These three houses were for tenant farmers.

Papa had amassed 650 acres of land, so a lot of plowing went on with seven mules, and two tractors planting, planting. Each tenant was allotted 10 to 14 acres of land to use as they wanted. They bought their own seed and fertilizer. Papa received one-fourth of their harvest in exchange for rent. They also worked extra for Papa and were paid. They could work on other farms for hire whenever they could. If Papa had to be away, the men could run the farm without any problem. During the winter months, Papa carried them financially. At the end of the year, they made a profit. He trusted them. Their wives had their own gardens and planted whatever they wanted. They did their own canning and quilting, like all the other women in the community. Mama got along well with the wives and children. We all played together, visited, went to the same school and church.

On Saturday afternoons, we went to downtown Columbia, Mississippi, because that was the thing to do. To me, we were all the same; there was no difference. I had no idea what tenant farmer meant as a child. Our lives were all alike. They helped Papa on the farm. We all worked. The tenant farmers were able to earn their own living and provide for their families, something the Department of Agriculture failed to help people accomplish after slavery. The importance of land ownership created a certain respect within the community. And being a successful and bigger farmer, Papa was known throughout the communities because of his farming, and his bricklaying and carpentry as well.

Hired Hands: Not Just Us Anymore

The cotton fields continued to grow and Papa hired hands for the day, which not only helped increase his productivity but also provided work for a lot of people. He always said it was a way that he could do good for others. At first, he hired only eight or ten hands from our community. He would give a ride to four or five of them in his pickup truck and the others would catch a ride every morning. That worked out for a couple of years, but as time went on and the cotton fields got bigger, more hands were needed. The old flatbed truck became a hauling truck for the fifteen or twenty additional hands Papa hired from Sumrall. They would gather in a certain spot in the morning and he would pick them up. The nine-mile ride normally took a good half hour to the fields and a half hour back.

That old engine woke us up every morning at sunrise as Papa was leaving and when he returned at sunset. In the mornings, except for Dan, Paul, and the tenant men, we were still in our beds. The hired hands jumped out or crawled sleepily out of that old truck wiping their eyes. The few who didn't eat at Mama's table clutched their brown-bag lunches. There was a yard full of folks ready to walk to the back field. A few would ride on the truck as Papa drove it to a good spot in the field. A long pole was built on the side of the truck or tractor trailer, with a chain and scale hanging from it to weigh the cotton just as it had been on the wagon years ago. Inside the cab of the truck, Papa had a wire-back tablet to keep records of every person's name and the weight of every sack of cotton. This activity was constant at different places down the cotton rows. The cotton sacks were of different lengths and sizes. The hired hands were of different body sizes, heights, skin color, ages; but all the adults dressed in overalls, Levis, long skirts with long-sleeve shirts, some women in pants, and all with straw hats. At the end of the day, they all knew exactly how many pounds they had picked. A big, brown barrel full of water was kept in the shade of a tree at the edge of the field. At mid-morning and mid-afternoon, Jimmy and I would go up to the house and get a big chunk of ice and bring it back to put in the barrel. Sometimes we carried a bucket of water with a dipper to the hands. Other times some of them would go over to the barrel to get their drink.

The going rate for picking cotton was $2.50 to $3.00 per hundred pounds; scraping cotton and thinning corn was $3.00 to $4.00 per day. At the end of the day and on Friday, everybody was paid in cash and all went home with big smiles on their faces. Papa's biggest year was 1952, with sixty bales of cotton at $418 a bale. I was thirteen years old and could not have been happier. With all the hired hands, working in the fields had changed since the days when Papa sold cotton for as little as sixteen cents a pound and a bale brought only thirty-five dollars.

Everyone was discouraged from picking trash and leaves even though it weighed more at the scale; but it was less at the gin where it was cleaned. There was no singing going on but everybody could talk if they wanted. A bad windstorm could blow through in late September and sweep through the harvest. When that cotton was picked, it was referred to as "storm cotton" at the gin because it was damaged. We always knew why we could not pick trash and leaves. Even picking cotton had to be done right. A good bale weighed 500 pounds and we picked three to five bales a day.

On hot days, I would stand out in the field with sweat running down my back. What a relief a cold drink of water from the barrel was. There were many people in the fields and so much cotton it looked like a scene in a picture. Long rows, straight and curved, on and on they went. Out of nowhere, a peach-sweetened breeze would pick up and warm, wet drops fall from above. The blue of the sky deepened and the clouds loomed bright until a huge shadow hung over the field. The scent of green filled the air and the freshest raindrops began to fall. These cloudbursts gave us an excuse to run to the cotton house, where we would dive into the cotton. We bounced and squirmed and screamed with delight, celebrating the afternoon's surprise. We dried off, our straw hats flopping, our jeans covered with lint. In the flurry of play, cotton surrounded us like soft snowflakes.

When we poked our heads out, it was as if the sun had never stopped — the heat rose and the cotton dried, and it was ready to be picked again. Every once in a while a small plane could be heard in the distance, and sometimes it crossed the sky high above us. I always looked up and watched it until it flew out of sight. I wondered where it had come from and where it was going. I dreamt about faraway places and riding on a big plane one day. Standing in the fields, I would drift off into a dream. But the only plane that flew through the blue skies over our house was a crop duster that the Morrises (white man) owned.

In Mama's Kitchen

Mama stepped lightly in a pair of old slide-in shoes and knee-high stockings. The dress was pink-and-white-flowered and hung loosely under a white apron with a big sash and pockets. Her white hair hung in soft curls combed to the left side of her face; it was yesterday's "Sunday-go-to-meeting" hairdo. She moved like comfort in a breeze, calmly going about the business of cooking, never getting frazzled, dropping things or rushing about.

The aroma of peach cobbler and chicken and dumplings was carried by the wind and reached the field hands. Stirred by their taste for good home-cooking, they walked single- and double-file along the fence up to the house, eyes and smiles widening. Any combination of a balanced meal was put together by Mama, or "Cousin Mae," some called her. Pots of collard greens and cornbread, black-eyed peas with okra, sweet corn, green beans and white potatoes, turnips, mustards, fried chicken, smothered pork chops. There was water, milk and an occasional soda pop to drink. There were no recipes or measuring of ingredients when she cooked. It all came with confidence and ease.

After lunch, groups of people lay across the front porch to nap. Others leaned against one of the big oak trees in the yard, hats covering their eyes. For an hour everything was still — no conversation, no movement. The occasional snore was ignored. The trek back to the field was energetic, made with renewed vigor. With their full stomachs, to the hands the cotton fields looked less daunting. In the late afternoon, close to quitting time, we could hear the whistling and cooing of birds, catch sight of rabbits leaping into the woods nearby — a good way to end the day. Year after year, most of the same hired hands came back to our fields — women and men, tall and short, lean and not so lean. One hundred acres was a lot of cotton; it was a consolation to us that we had their help.

Farmers shared a common bond: farm life. They'd talk about their farms and what was going on with them, and how they might improve things. Many evenings they'd sit on the front porch, talking with Papa, colored men and white men alike — they were all in the same boat. The land bonded them; segregation was not an issue. The land, and respect for each other, was the glue that held them together.

Papa sat on the front porch in the early evenings, chewing tobacco and spitting juice across the porch onto the grass. Mama dipped her snuff and spat too, recollecting how she used to pick 400 pounds of cotton a day in the early years. We kids sat on the edge of the porch, listening to them talk, but also watching the lightning bugs and hearing the noises of the night. Working hard made us strong and gave us a sense of ourselves. It made us independent of whites because we knew we would always survive.

Building chimneys and small frame houses was Papa's other job. He always worked, was always busy. In his old run-over brown shoes, faded long-sleeved blue shirt, blue overalls and straw hat with the sides tilted up, he built chimneys for a lot of folks in a lot of communities. During the early years, a chimney cost $5.00 to lay the bricks, and building a small house cost $1.50 an hour. Papa had been taught by Mama's oldest brother-in-law, Uncle Hark, when Papa was courting Mama from 1912 to 1917. Papa continued building until he got too old.

He built our house in 1922-23, hauling discarded lumber with his mule and wagon from the local sawmill, digging up stumps from land the Great Southern Lumber Company had cleared. For us, working in the fields did not seem as hard as it actually was because Papa said you'll always have something if you work hard. So when he told us to go out to the fields on Saturday mornings and clear them of small stumps, we knew he would pay us and we'd have spending money. When Papa told us how things used to be, it gave me confidence. I knew that things had improved over the years and that with hard work we could always make a living.

The Special Field

Across the road in front of the house was a field of potatoes and vegetables, much like Mama's garden, but bigger. It was a special field for the needy. It was planted every year, and anyone could come and get the food. Papa planted potatoes, peas, beans, greens, okra, and corn — everything good. Colored as well as whites came, carrying their burlap sacks, some walking, some in wagons with a mule that maybe needed hay, which was also provided. At church it would be announced, and by word of mouth the word got out. When I asked an older brother how long ago that field had first been planted, he said it was during the Great Depression. Papa read about Adam C. Powell, Sr., a preacher in New York who had a soup kitchen during the depression, and he was impressed by that. Papa felt that if you could help people, you should do it. His way was to grow food they could pick themselves for their families. A journal called *The Messenger* was published by a man named A. Phillip Randolph, who spoke out about the military draft at the very time Papa was drafted into the army in 1918. An article about the soup kitchen was in that journal.

Sharecropping

On one of those evenings when Papa sat on the porch after supper and a long day in the fields, he talked about having been up to Indianola, Mississippi, visiting Mama's brother, Uncle Sonny. Chewing tobacco and spitting juice, he told Mama about the real Delta, hotter and more humid, where farms that were plantations were owned by whites and where colored folks were worked to the bone. There were hundreds of acres, he said, but describing how the sharecroppers lived was what Papa talked about the most. He'd shake his head and say, "I don't know how they do it."

We sat there quietly, listening. Uncle Sonny was the principal of an elementary school and his wife taught school there. His work ethic was just as strong as Papa's. Work hard, get a good education, be sure of yourself, and do not let others deter you. He would drive Papa around the countryside where rundown shacks seemed to be everywhere and where hardly any gardens grew. Hundreds of colored folks bent over in the fields, sweating in the hot sun, colored folks like us. Unlike the same hard work we shared that nourished and bonded us to other farmers and landowners we knew, these people labored harder than we ever had and for a man who didn't even treat them right.

Papa had told us how his grandpappy Elias had been a slave until he was 14 years old. Determined to be free, after two or three attempts he finally succeeded in running away. The marks on his back from years of beatings always remained, but his spirit could not be broken. Freedom was inside of him. The land taught us how to survive. There was nothing more important.

The farm was always lively — people everywhere, walking around, riding an old mule, or sitting in wagons going down the road. Cows wandered down from the meadows, chickens clucked, dogs barked. Activity, excitement, adventure. I remember these things and more, and how they guided me throughout my life. The times were busy then, the times were good. They helped me keep grounded, brought me peace of mind, and taught me not to be afraid.

Those farming years were busy in every community. Downtown Columbia was bustling, active and busy, with people everywhere. Groups of women — Mama, Miss Ella, Miss Mary, and Aunt Sang — got together to make quilts at one another's houses. In later years, they went to the schoolhouse on Saturday mornings to make their quilts.

Each woman would be seated across from another, usually four to a group, with the lining of the quilt suspended on a wide, man-made rack. Each woman brought her own scrap material and filling. It was socializing at its best, as was the canning up at the schoolhouse when the women got together there.

Pleasure Foods

SWEET POTATOES

One of my favorite memories is of Papa baking sweet potatoes in the ashes of the fireplace. When they were roasted, we ate them with a big chunk of the homemade butter Mama made, along with a big glass of milk. We savored this treat by the fireplace in the early evenings. They were good served plain, but sometimes Mama opened up a jar of peaches, pears, plums, or grapes during the winter and served them with the sweet potatoes for lunch or supper.

From late March to mid–April, we planted our sweet potatoes through a process called potato beds. Those were small furrows made with a hoe or plow, into which we laid the potatoes down in a line, side by side, in rows about three feet long. Once they sprouted, the grass started to invade, and out came the hoe, scraping out the grass the same way we scraped between the cotton stalks. At harvest time from late September to the first week in October, we could see the potatoes breaking the soil and moles crawling under the surface, cracking the soil open. That meant it was time to plow up the potatoes. Finally, it was time to pick them by hand, put them into piles and then into large buckets, and load them onto the wagon (later, we used the pickup truck).

Most everything was ready for harvest by August every year — that wonderful cotton, especially, and the sweet potatoes, which were grown mostly for our personal use. Mama would can many jars and Papa would build a hay and dirt pyramid, which was a big mound that had layers of sweet potatoes, then hay, and then dirt, each of these alternated until the pyramids reached three feet high. The pyramid preserved the sweet potatoes so that in the winter months of December and January we could go outside and get big red sweet potatoes to bake or fix some other way whenever we wanted them.

SUGARCANE

Sugarcane was another of our pleasure foods. Walking through Papa's sugarcane patch, down one row and then the other, we would look for the first sign of cracking soil and a green leaf folded over, pushing its way up and out as if reaching for daylight. The leaves would open almost as soon as sunlight drew them up toward the sky. It would be the first of April when our sprouts poked through but late September before we could go out to the cane patch, cut down a stalk of sugarcane with a hacksaw or a big knife, peel the leaves off, break the stalk into smaller pieces, peel off the outer covering, and finally bite off a mouthful of crunchy, juicy sweet, delicious cane. What an experience! When the juice ran down the sides of my mouth, I just pulled up the hem of my dress to wipe it off and spit out the pulp as I went along, repeating this process until my belly stuck out, big with sweet juice.

The stalks were usually green, occasionally reddish. Ours was the best climate for sugarcane, ranging from high heat and heavy rainfall to dry weather. New sprouts sprang from the stubble and produced a second crop even without planting them. After stripping the stalks and loading them onto a wagon or pickup truck, Papa took his cane over to Mr. John Watts because he had the best cane mills.

Thanksgiving or November was the time for making syrup, and sometimes the men were outside doing this until midnight. Once the cane was processed, no exact time was set for heating the cane juice and skimming it. The men just stood around, or sat on wooden crates, chewing tobacco, sipping whiskey, telling white lies, and enjoying the whole process. Some people came by just to drink the fresh juice before it got to the furnace. A gallon of juice cost thirty-five cents.

We stored gallons of syrup in the smokehouse and in the small pantry of the kitchen where Mama kept her canned jars and vegetables.

Papa sold the syrup to some people and gave it away to others. At one time, he had his own cane mill down by the old gravel pit, but he wasn't any good at making syrup and he knew it, so he took his cane over to John Watts, whom we all knew made syrup better than anybody. The sugarcane was stored in straw and dirt banks by November, just as our sweet potatoes were.

PEACHES

Late May to October was the best time for peaches. They were never stored in a cold place because that held their flavor back. And if picked too soon, they wouldn't be sweet. Papa planted an acre of peach trees near the house that looked like a vast orchard to me when I was a child. Each tree was so loaded with big, blush-colored balls it seemed like they would topple over. Sometimes we ate them right there, in the shade of the trees, without even washing them. Or we'd sit on the edge of the porch, tossing the pits across the grass and into the nearby geraniums and gladiolas. Half of the trees gave us peaches that were smaller but noticeably sweeter. I'd eat so many my stomach ached.

GRAPES

The best thing to eat at the end of the day was grapes—juicy and round, smooth-skinned and shiny like pearls. We'd pull the vines apart in the one spot where we could fit under the big arbor, all shaded and cool, and fill our mouths with those sweet little glorious things.

Papa planted the seeds directly under a big, circular overhead scaffold that he had built with poles in the middle for vines to climb and break through. Eventually, they spread and covered the scaffold like a canopy and draped all the way down to the ground. It was as big as the room of a house under there. I never washed a grape back then and it was good old refreshing eating.

STRAWBERRIES

My first and most vivid memory of strawberries was seeing Grandma at the top of the hill, walking down the road to our house

Mama standing on the steps of our porch enjoying watermelon in 1950.

when I was three or four years old. Grandma was the only one I knew who had strawberries. She wore long, soft, colorful print dresses with a white apron just as long that had two big pockets and a wide sash tied in the back. In the pockets were some perfectly round, light brown tea cakes, wrapped in a handmade white towel. From her hand would swing a basket of freshly picked strawberries.

Jimmy and I would start running to meet her. Once we got close, Grandma stopped, put down her basket, and stretched out her arms for us to fall into. A big, wet kiss on my face was next, and just as soon, I'd wipe it off when her face was turned. Jimmy and I started eating the strawberries before we got back to the house.

WATERMELONS AT LAST

After church on late Sunday afternoons, after Mama and Papa had gone to visit the sick and the shut-ins, we'd come home, change into our everyday clothes, and down to the watermelon patch we'd go. The sun would be setting and shining through the trees at the end of the rows.

The base of a tree was the best place to sit and eat watermelon. This was after I mastered the art of thumping it and listening for a certain sound. That was when you knew it was ripe. Bursting it on the roots of the tree, sitting down with chunks of irregular pieces everywhere, and scooping out a big piece with my bare hands—red, juicy and sweet—was as pure as heaven. There was no cutting it up in small cubes, eating it with a fork and preventing the juice from running down the sides of your mouth. Jimmy and Myrtis were in on this treat.

Autumn

During the months of late September through most of November, the leaves on our oak trees turned the prettiest crimson, scarlet, burnt orange, sienna, amber, and gold—a real jewel box of colors. Who would mind the job of raking up the leaves with so much to look at? Besides, a big pile of leaves was just perfect for jumping right into the middle and for stretching out your arms and legs and looking up at the clear blue sky to watch the pearly white clouds roll by. Imagine a more comfortable way to dream if you can! And at that time of year, what I dreamt about was Mama's syrup tea cakes. Her red bread was good, too. With a big glass of fresh cow's milk, there was no better eating.

Back in the Barnyard

Depending on which way the wind blew, there was no doubt that the big old A-frame building was down the road. Without seeing anything in the yard or hearing any sounds, you knew that there just had to be hogs, or mules, or cows and chickens nearby. The hogs had the real scent. The combination of odors that wafted through the air could be overwhelming for the weak at heart or city folks. But us country folks got used to the barn and barnyard smells.

The hog pen had two small stalls with a long wooden trough right next to the gate. The hog food was poured into the trough. Those hogs could be heard from all over the barnyard. You'd think they'd never had anything to eat from the noise they made. If you had the nerve to go in, you'd be standing knee-deep in soupy mud, dirt, and hog poop, inhaling the most disgusting, revolting odor. Weak stomachs could look in from the barnyard fence and simply wonder what was inside. The two milking stalls stood on the right side of the barn, with an enclosed storage area at the end of the stalls. A little hay and other things were kept there. Against the outside wall was storage for the tractor and equipment. From front to back, a wide, open breezeway separated the right side from the left. The left side had four stalls for mules. Other mules were outside in the barnyard and rotated with the mules in the stalls. All the mules had names—Sam, who was smaller, Doc, Nell, Tommy, Rock, Old Emma, and Duke, the crazy rodeo horse.

One time Paul decided to show off on Duke, the crazy black rodeo horse. Before he could get on him good old Duke took off, with Paul's foot stuck in the stirrup. That horse dragged him almost to the back road behind the house, until it hit a big limb. For days Paul had more pain and soreness than he'd ever imagined. He couldn't tell Mama and Papa because he had been showing off.

Old Emma was our pet mule, old and too tired to plow. Dan tried to teach Jimmy and me to ride her with one of Mama's old folded quilts on her back. He'd help me get up on her and lead her around and around. But every time Old Emma bent her head down, I would slide right off. Up on her again, I'd start over until I learned to stay on. Jimmy tried a few times and gave up altogether. By the time I was eight, I could ride behind Dan, going fast on the mule or the smaller horse.

The outside covered wall along the mule stalls was lined with four chicken coops. The top and front doors were wood and the sides were chicken wire. A little straw nest was in one corner, and every day we had to check for eggs. The chickens were fed with corn and grain for weeks before they were killed to eat.

Mama's chicken coop was nothing like Aunt Sang's, because she raised little chicks. Killing a chicken to me was terrible, and there were only two ways to do it. If you wrung its neck, the chicken would run around afterwards. Chopping off the head on a stump with an ax was even worse. The blood spurted everywhere and the body would still move. That was one job I did not like doing. After they were finally dead, hot scalding water had to be poured over the body and the feathers plucked. Feathers would be flying all around, which meant more scalding water. Gutting the chicken was not too bad because there was not much inside. By then, chicken and dumplings started to look real good.

The Hay Loft

Every now and then one of the cows got out of the barnyard gate. It was a funny picture to see us running around, trying to steer a cow back to the barnyard. I knew the cow was playing with us, and it was always funny to me. I laughed continuously until it was back in the barnyard.

The loft was my special place and I would climb to it on the ladder between the cow stalls and the enclosed section on the right side of the stalls. Half of the loft was a covered floor, and the other half had open beams where you could look down and see the mules below. The loft was open from the front to back just as if it was on the ground level. In the late afternoon before I was big enough to pick cotton, I'd fill my pockets full of pecans or plums—or one of Mama's tea cakes—and off I'd go to the barn loft.

I'd sit on the edge of the opening, looking out over the barnyard, over the field across the road—waving at the passing cars and trucks stirring up dust—and taking in Mama's pretty lilies, azaleas and the evergreen junipers in the front yard. In the barnyard was a storage building, just like the ones in the cotton fields. It had corn and a little hay in it. A big, circular wooden water barrel about three feet high and at least five feet across watered everything in the barn and yard. Outside the yard was the almighty windmill, which provided water for the barnyard and had a pump for drinking water. The wind blew and the big blades rotated from a center shaft, pumping water. Windmills in the neighborhood were scarce. I thought only white folks had windmills. I would climb our big windmill just outside the barnyard and look all the way to China.

Hog-Killing Time

The other big event that took place was hog killing. The ones to be killed were kept in a separate pen and fed. One month before the hogs were killed, Dan and Paul would cook sweet potatoes, corn, and wheat in a big wash pot and feed the hogs. A small amount of red lye was mixed in a five-gallon bucket of feed to clean the hogs of worms. They were also fed cucumbers, watermelons and food from the table. When I was big enough, I would sometimes help feed the hogs in the early morning with Dan and Paul.

Papa killed hogs during the full moon. This was the end of the fourth quarter, which came in September and lasted through late March. If they were killed at any other time, the bacon, when fried, would curl up in the Crisco cooking oil. This was one of the indications that the hog had been killed out of season. The fatback would be rubbery and flabby and would not taste as good as it would have if the hog had been killed at the right time of year.

In the back barnyard, outside the fence and down the hill, was a little creek that ran for miles on either side of the road and the road with the bridge across it just down from the house. One area there was used to first clean the small intestines of the hogs in the fresh clean water before Mama got to them.

Papa would kill one big hog that he had especially fattened up just for the lard contents. This was always a female hog, or sow. He got many gallon containers of fat from that one sow. Most he kept for himself, but a few gallons were given to Uncle Luther and a can or two to other families around the neighborhood.

The one other hog that was killed was for our personal use. Papa killed that hog by shooting it. He, Dan and Paul would then scald it with hot water to make it easier to remove the hair by scraping if off with a sharp knife. Then the hog was split open and its insides were gutted out. The chitterlings, or small intestines, were removed. They were filled with fat, waste products, and digested food. Once the chitterlings were cleaned, we ate them either fried or boiled. The texture was rubbery, but not if they were fried. The ham was cured in the smokehouse.

Sausage was prepared by Mama with her meat grinder. The section of meat used for sausage was put in the grinder and ground up. This ground meat was also used for hamburger meat. Seasoning was added to complete the preparation — a little pepper, a dash of salt, and usually sage. The casing for the sausage was the small intestine. After it was thoroughly cleaned, it was looped over the mound of the grinder. Then the meat was stuffed inside and a handle turned by hand, creating those long pieces of sausage that would later be cut up into cooking-size pieces.

Pork chop sections were from the loin area of the hog. Mama cooked them in many different ways: fried, baked, stuffed with some other kind of meat, or smothered in brown gravy. The possibilities were endless. Bacon sections came from the outer layer and included the rind, or skin, of the hog. This area was sliced thin, usually less than an eighth of an inch thick. Pork skins—cracklings—also came from the outer layer of the hog and they too included the rind. They were sliced about the same size, but with a little lean and fat. This allowed Papa to remove all the fat left between the skin and the lean portion to make lard. The skin was cut up into cubes about one-inch thick.

Hog head cheese was made of meat from the head of the hog cut off the bones and ground up. It was mixed mainly with cornmeal, vinegar, hot sauce, salt, pepper, and spices. The mixture was put into a meat-loaf type of pan and placed in the refrigerator to set until it solidified like gelatin; then it was cut into slices and served.

After Dan and Paul were drafted into the army in 1953, Papa took his hogs down to the slaughterhouse out on Highway 24 near Hilltop Grocery. Later, all he had to do was pick up the cleaned, cut up, labeled and packaged meat the slaughterhouse had prepared. Of course, he had to pay for it, but it saved him a whole lot of time and energy.

Before Electricity and Running Water

Our house and its furnishings fill my memories with warmth. The linoleum on the dining room and kitchen floors was brownish tan; the living room linoleum had a pattern of blue roses. A kerosene lamp stood on a table in every room. Every one of those lamps sat right on top of a white, yellow, blue, or green doily. Each of the doilies had been starched so stiff with white flour paste that it stood up on its own — that is, after Myrtis had ironed them with the old cast iron that she had heated over hot ashes in the fireplace, or on the wood-burning cast-iron stove in the kitchen.

Sometimes at night, especially during the colder months, Papa would put a half-bucket of peanuts in the ashes of the fireplace in his and Mama's room to parch them. He'd put a couple of big pine logs on the fire just as everybody was going to bed; the logs would burn most of the night, usually needing only a little paper or kindling to restart in the morning. He always kept a small can of kerosene in the kitchen just in case it was needed to restart the fire.

Mama and Papa's bedroom was off the front porch and had a fireplace. The wooden post bed had a matching four-drawer chest and a dresser with a sunken center and a big round mirror. A kerosene lamp on the fireplace mantle and one on the dresser lit the room. Right behind Mama and Papa's room was another, small, girls' bedroom and it had Papa's old trunk and a wardrobe in it. On the left side of Papa and Mama's room was the living room with a blue couch, two chairs, two end tables, and the piano. A front door opened to the porch. The door to the left of a small hallway off my parents' room opened to my brothers' bedrooms; the end of the hall opened to the dining room and kitchen, with one last brothers' bedroom to the left off the dining room. Our old Victrola sat on the chest in that room.

All the dressers and chests in the bedrooms had lamps on them. Mama's dining room set had a long and short buffet, a lattice and glass china cabinet, and a big table that would seat six grown folks. When my older brothers were little, Papa bought that set for Mama from a white woman who lived on a farm quite a ways from our house. A small icebox sat in the left corner of our dining room.

Our kitchen had its own fireplace. Darlene, Jimmy, Myrtis and I ate at a wooden table Papa had built along the left wall. A cast-iron, four-burner wood stove was not only the best to cook on, Mama would say, but also provided additional heat in the wintertime. A small door on the right side of the kitchen led to a closet-sized area for storing Mama's canning on shelves. And a big bucket was in the corner on the floor, a "slop bucket" of leftover food for the hogs.

Cotton filled all the mattresses on the beds. Mama's bleached white flour sacks were sewn into squares with yellow, green, and blue embroidered hems for sheets and pillowcases. The handmade quilts were filled with scrap cotton. Ironing clothes with a heavy cast iron put heavy creases in Dan and Paul's Levis and Papa's white Sunday-go-to-church shirts. Myrtis was real good at ironing and did most of it. When I got big enough, I would iron sheets and pillowcases and my little cotton blouses and skirts for school. So did Jimmy.

On the back porch, Papa had built a long shelf across one open end, and it held the drinking-water bucket and dipper, a face-and-hand wash basin, a bar of Ivory soap, and a little container of baking soda with which to brush our teeth. Just off the porch was the well, with a pulley overhead and a bucket attached to draw water. The well was circular and made of cement, about twelve inches wide and five feet high. It was our main source of water for drinking, cooking, cleaning, and washing. A chain-link fence with a front center gate and a back gate surrounded the house. Outside the front yard loomed two big oak trees.

Washing clothes was a big outside ritual. A cast-iron wash pot full of water sat up off the ground on blocks and bricks under a roaring fire, and we boiled everything from Mama's homemade sheets and pillowcases to Papa's, Dan's and Paul's overalls and Levis. Lye soap, with a little baking soda added to the pot, cleaned everything. One tub was for washing and scrubbing on an old washboard; the other tub was for rinsing. The clotheslines were always full of snow-white sheets blowing in the wind and absorbing the fresh smell of the sun.

Outside the backyard fence was the smokehouse built of blocks. It was about eight by ten feet in size, with open beams, a dirt floor, and a half wall of shelves. It was used for curing and smoking meat. A rope with hooks and chains hung from the ceiling; this would hold the ham for curing over a pit in the smoke of wood burning. When Papa and Mama weren't home, Jimmy and I would go into the smokehouse, rip off a piece of ham, and gorge ourselves with delight. Curing a ham had taken almost two weeks, but we did our work in short time.

Canning took up a lot of the summer months. The annual beets, sweet peas, snap beans, green beans, black-eyed peas, and corn on the cob came from Mama's garden and the peaches from the orchard. We sat on the front porch shelling peas, snapping beans, and scraping sweet corn. Mama canned everything. We kids gathered, washed, picked, shucked, scraped, and chopped.

The Outdoor Toilet

Ours was considered a cut above the rest because it was a two-seater. The wooden structure, with its tin roof and interior big enough for two, stood outside the back fence close to the field. The wood was gray and looked like barn siding; the center door set it off. Sears Roebuck catalogue pages and sometimes an old Alden's catalogue were our toilet tissue. Chamber pots sat under all the beds and had to be emptied into the outdoor toilet, cleaned every morning, and placed back under the beds for nighttime. We took turns— Jimmy and Myrtis and me — with that most personal of duties.

A Brighter House

In 1948, when I was all of nine years old, something wonderful changed our nights and days forever. When electricity came to the house, a city-like way of life began to take place. A little flip of a switch and the whole house would light up. I was so excited that at nighttime when Mama and Papa were off visiting or gone to prayer meeting on Wednesday nights I would turn on every light and go out to the road to look at the wonder of our house — every window ablaze with a new kind of light.

Electricity ran the electric refrigerator, electric iron, the little black and white TV, a couple of electric table lamps in addition to the ceiling lights, hot and cold running water for the kitchen and bathroom sinks, the hot water heater with a pilot light that would go out sometimes and which I would always relight. The TV had only two or three channels and we watched *Ed Sullivan, Arthur Godfrey, Dinah Shore,* and the *Nat King Cole Show. Godzilla* and *King Kong* made up my late-night entertainment after everybody else had gone to bed. Papa would be asleep almost as soon as he sat down. Mama would get up and go to bed after a short time. Darlene, Jimmy and Myrtis would go to bed after the popular shows went off the air. There was not much daytime TV watching because we were in the fields or in school.

The other wonderful thing that happened when electricity came was that Papa built an addition to our house. Our original seven-room house had been built in 1923 and now we had three more rooms— a regular-sized bedroom with a fireplace; a smaller child's bedroom, about six by eight feet; and a bathroom and closet. The smaller room was mine — I had my own room, so knew I was a big girl now. It held only a twin bed and a small table, with just enough room to walk on one side of the bed, but it had three windows and a lot of light. The closet was next to the fireplace. Darlene and Myrtis slept in the other new bedroom. Jimmy slept in the original house, in a small room right off Mama and Papa's bedroom, which used to belong to my older sisters, Carzella and Loretta, before they left home.

Our Daily Chores

At the end of cotton-picking season, there would be "scrap" cotton used for Mama's quilting. Papa would have us go out and pick it for her. Sometimes a couple of women in the community, Miss Ella or Mary, would come along and they would cut out scraps of different shapes and sew them together, making a pretty colorful pattern. By the mid–1950s, the schoolhouse had an area where a group of eight women could gather around a suspended rack with four on each side and make quilts. Each woman brought her own scrap material and filling. Mama, Aunt Sang, Miss Ella, and Mary were the main ones who got together at the school and at each other's homes.

Canning would be done up at the schoolhouse in a big room off the cafeteria. It had modern equipment that could bottle the food in a short time. All we had to do was gather the vegetables. They could be washed up there and put in jars. We did the heavy cleaning: shucking corn, snapping beans, shelling peas.

There were many activities that went on at our house when I was little — and I got into enough of them. We had a big pecan tree in a field behind the house and it bore a lot of pecans. There were some little boys in the neighborhood who would cut through the back woods and help themselves, but for us just eating them was good enough. Mama would save a half sack to do her Christmas baking and she would give pecans away.

One time, about a month or so before Christmas, while peeking in and out of cabinets and the wardrobe, our curiosity got us into trouble. Mama and Papa were over at Aunt Sang's house and Darlene and I were in Dan and Paul's bedroom. We noticed what looked like the corner of a burlap sack sticking out from under the mattress. That was just enough for us to pull the covers back and move the mattress. It was easy because the cotton-filled mattress was light and soft. The surprise was a sack full of pecans! I got a knife and poked a hole in one side of the sack, just big enough to get my hand in. After that, every single day when Mama and Papa were on the front porch or out in the yard, we'd go in and grab a big handful from the sack to eat outside. When it was time to cook cakes for the holidays, Mama learned she didn't have enough pecans. And she knew who ate them. She called me in the room and pulled the sack out onto the floor. It was pitiful how many we'd eaten.

The routine was to go out in the yard and get that perfectly long, thin, green switch. Gathering the folds of my dress to one side, Mama swung the switch over my legs. Those stinging, painful licks were enough to stop my pecan-stealing habit. Papa didn't whip us, only Mama, but the one time he did, Jimmy and I made it up beforehand to cry real loud with the first lick. He used his hand, and he never got in more than three licks. I would scream as loud as I could and Papa would stop — but it really didn't hurt.

Another time, while rummaging in Mama's chest of drawers, I came upon what looked like chocolate candy and broke off three little squares, gave Darlene one, and took the other two. We stood there and ate it all on the spot. Mama didn't have to ask who took them — it was obvious in a few hours, and she didn't even whip us. What we thought was candy was Ex-lax. We spent a lot of time in the toilet.

How to milk the cow was taught by my brother Paul. It was not a chore expected of me, but it was one I liked to do. At ten or eleven, I would crawl out my bedroom window, go around to the back porch, and wash my hands and face from a washbowl. Soap and a towel hanging from a nail were nearby. At first, I used my clinched hand on that old cow's tits, until Paul showed me how to use my thumb and four fingers, squeezing and pulling a little. The milk came pouring out. Sitting on a little stool and holding that bucket between my knees was another thing. At first, that old cow would step back, knocking over half my milk. But pulling on the tits the right way stopped any kicking. I would have the milk in the icebox for Mama before she got up in the morning.

A Joy Ride

One day when I was twelve years old and Darlene was nine, Mama and Papa had gone up to Grandma's house. Looking for something to do, we girls decided to take the truck and go to the store. Of course, the store was just a destination, somewhere to go to and come home from. The fun part was driving the truck. So I went to get the keys, which were always hanging on a nail right by the fireplace mantel. But I discovered the gas gauge was on empty. I figured we could get some gas from the tractor.

Out to the barn we went. I got a small hose and a bucket, opened the gas tank on the tractor, and siphoned out a bucket full of gas. I carried the bucket back to the truck and poured it into the tank with a piece of cardboard I used as a funnel. It worked, and off to the store we could go. Papa wouldn't know that we stole the gas, and he wouldn't show up at the store because we had his truck — we knew we were safe.

Darlene and I were on the road in the pickup on the way to the store and we passed an old man driving a car. Since he was driving close to my side of the road, I tried to avoid his car and ended up driving straight into a ditch. There we sat, the two of us thinking, *Now what do we do?* "Okay, let's walk back to the house and get a rope and the tractor to pull the truck out of the ditch," I said. Darlene agreed, and we set out walking. When we got up to the barnyard and didn't see anyone, I got the rope. The key was always left in the tractor, and

Paul had taught me how to drive it when I was ten years old. Darlene climbed on behind me and we got out of there. On the way back to the truck, we passed a couple of cars on the gravel road, but I didn't move over too far. We were high up on that tractor, for everyone to see for as far as we could see. This time, they had to do the moving over.

I backed the tractor near the truck and stopped. I tied one end of the rope to the back of the tractor and the other end to the bumper of the truck. Somehow it held together. Darlene guided the steering wheel until I pulled the truck onto the road and we parked it. We drove the tractor back to the house, still with no one around. Then we walked back to the truck and went to the store. I don't even remember what we bought — maybe a candy bar or a soda pop. After working in the fields all week, Saturday afternoons were the perfect time to go to the store. The point was to pull up there all by ourselves in the truck.

Though I knew how to drive, I was allowed to do it only occasionally because Dan and Paul did most of the driving. Besides, I was too young to get a license. When Dan and Paul got older, by the time they were in tenth grade, Papa bought a car for them. They could go wherever they wanted without having to ask Papa for his pickup truck or to ask for the family car, which was mostly for going to church, the store, visiting, or downtown on Saturday afternoons to socialize and be seen.

Mama couldn't drive an inch. She didn't hunt with my uncles — Sonny, Shug, and Tobie — as her sisters did, and she didn't fix things around the house. Papa tried once to teach her how to drive, but she seemed to have an aversion to things mechanical. (Or was it a resistance to activities deemed "manly"?) When Mama got behind the wheel, that old four-door sedan would just jerk itself to a halt. It had a stick shift, and Mama never got the hang of it. All she had to do was get the car from the yard out to the gravel road in front of the house, but she couldn't make it that far even while mashing down the gas pedal. She never tried again.

A Snake

One time when I was about seven, I was walking across the old cotton field behind the house. There were rows of old, dried-up cotton and stalks, dirt and leaves, and trash. All of a sudden I saw a brown snake, the same color as the dirt. Not a sound came from that snake as it wiggled over the ground, but I caught it just in time; down came my stick, right on top of it, as hard as I could hit. I always carried that stick with me when walking by myself. The snake didn't move, so I hit it three or four more times to make sure it was dead.

When I got back up to the house, I couldn't wait to tell Mama. "I killed a snake. He was big and brown and I wasn't too scared of him. He didn't move, so I beat him to death." She just told me to be careful when I go walking around the fields, or in the barnyard. Any snake was to be killed as far as I was concerned. There was no such thing as good snakes or bad snakes. They all were to be killed, even the little green ones.

Gone Fishing

Going fishing with Aunt Sang, Mama's sister, was a real escape and Jimmy and I always went along. There was a lot we had to take with us—the fishing pole with line and hooks, a small bucket with earthworms for bait, a small shovel to dig for more worms, an old straw hat, shoes with good soles on them, and overalls or Levis with a long-sleeved shirt to keep the bugs off us and prevent too much bruising from blackberry vines and dogwood limbs while walking through the woods. Aunt Sang always brought a few of her famous chicken sandwiches and bottles of soda pop, usually grape and orange. A lunch like this was a special treat for us because Mama never packed us sandwiches for school. Papa gave us lunch money every day to buy a hot meal.

The woods might have been only a mile from the house, but the scent of cedars and pines gave them the enchantment of a faraway forest. To get there we walked through three fields behind the house — an acre of peach trees, a couple of acres of sugarcane, and a big cotton field that went all the way to the fence that separated Papa's land from Mr. Harris's. About halfway to our fishing spot was a grapevine winding and coiling its way over a small, ragged wooden structure. I'm sure Papa had built it years earlier so that the vine could run wild.

At the edge of the cotton field a gravel road separated it from another cotton field that went right up to the woods. Old persimmon and hickory nut trees were in abundance, as were shorter, frailer trees loaded with bitter crab apples. Sometimes there'd be a green apple tree, but the apples never tasted good. At the end of summer, they would start falling to the ground and rotting in the underbrush, giving off a cider-like fragrance of fermentation that was almost intoxicating.

The walk was delicious, offering blueberries and mulberries all along the wooded path, and occasionally even dewberries. If I saw a little green snake slithering along, I would pick up a piece of wood and kill it. Since I knew I could do this, I was never afraid of them, not even a moccasin snake curled up in the woods, or a rattler that I might not even see but knew by the sound of the horny rings at the end of his tail. Once in a while his delicate skin would turn up, shed and abandoned along the path. Snakes were never a reason not to walk somewhere, nor were lizards, spiders, or hawks, which, along with wasps and bees, flies and rats, were a part of outdoor life — to be balanced with the sweet aromas and visual splendors that also surrounded us. Just the same, the wriggle of a snake meant that Jimmy would run and catch up with Mama and Aunt Sang for a short time.

There were many creatures to look at in the woods. Rabbits darting by in the blink of an eye. Golden honeycombs glowing more visibly than hornet nests. Gnats and butterflies flitting through patches of sun, and hummingbirds skirting from branch to branch, their long, sword-like beaks leading them to every blossom.

Sometimes, strolling along, I'd walk into a trap without knowing it — the outer rings of a gossamer web that had been hidden in the shade but was now shimmering in the sun. Sometimes the fat-bellied, long-legged web-maker would catch our attention. We loved to watch the victims, stuck and tormented, caught in the web—flies, for example, which were everywhere, a fact of life in summer. Mama used to warn us that insects would eat anything. Silkworms ate the mulberry leaves and termites helped themselves to the wood. Flies got the swatter, but the little red-dotted ladybugs that ate the greens in Mama's garden were too cute to kill. Ladybugs made wishes come true.

With lips and tongues blue from berries, Mama and Aunt Sang would walk and talk, laughing and enjoying each other's company, while Jimmy and I strolled through the woods. We never went down to the riverbank at any other time (especially since none of us could swim), and we never took the same path twice. Aunt Sang had different bait than we had, which was just earthworms. She had chicken liver to catch catfish and lizard-like "puppy-dogs" she found under logs in damp sections in the woods. Earthworms were dug up during the day and used more frequently, and small crawfish were raked from puddles of water. Minnows were also among Aunt Sang's bait collection.

Once at the river, we sat with the bait on the hook in the water, waiting—and waiting for hours it seemed—for the line to start shaking, pulling, jerking. Jimmy and I complained of being hungry, and Aunt Sang calmly told us to be quiet, the noise would scare the fish away. I figured the fish could hear. Mama just said, "Shush up." Finally something tugged on the line, or at least I thought so. My pole wiggled and pulled, bobbed and swayed, and I thought of that fat, juicy worm at the end of my hook and that pretty little lure that Aunt Sang brought me from Uncle Shug's shop. I just knew this was the big one, or maybe even just the one I would catch that day. Jimmy's pole arched over mine, at times crossed it. If you hold onto your pole and not let it drift, you'll get what you want. The next thing I knew, Aunt Sang had both poles, one in each hand, and two fish were flying through the air into our bucket.

We had fresh trout that night for supper. Whether the catch was trout, perch, bass, or catfish, we cleaned it outside, removing the scales with a sharp knife. We filled a black, cast-iron frying pan halfway with lard—the fat from our hogs—and fried the fish with salt and pepper. Mama served them with turnip greens and cornbread, baked sweet potatoes and a big glass of fresh milk. If any of our older brothers just happened to be home on furlough when the fish was fried, especially Boy Noah, they ate the tail and the head along with the whole fish.

Papa's Picnic

When I was around eight years old, every year or so at the end of the summer when the weather got a little cooler, Papa organized a big picnic down in the pasture behind the barn, near the fish pond. The pond was just beyond the little creek that ran under the bridge across the road and through the pasture, a good 250 feet behind the barn (so no smells from the barn came down to the pond). The pasture had a lot of trees, but the area near the pond was cleared somewhat and leveled off with grass, so we had a place to play. The pond made the picnic fun because lots of people liked to fish. Near the road, bricks were laid in a circle to build an open fire and prop up a cast-iron pot for deep-frying the day's catch. One old man who could make a barbecue pit out of a big metal barrel set one up for Papa and did the cooking as well.

Everybody came: toddlers, hobblers, teenagers, and just plain everybody. The trees kept everyone shaded from the sun, and honeysuckle vines covered the pasture with their sweet fragrance. Blueberry bushes grew beyond the pond, closer to Barry and Vera's house.

People sat anywhere and everywhere — on tree stumps created by Papa, on crates, on tree limbs (for the young people), and even on upside-down buckets. Others just plopped down on the grass. Some of the women who were a little prissy put their quilts on the ground. I could smell the fresh grass and before long the back pasture was filled with the aroma of fish frying and hamburgers grilling on the open fire.

Soda bottles people had pulled out of a big tin washtub of ice were popped open.

Children ran and laughed as they played. Yoyos flew up and down, in and out, and small rubber balls on elastic string bounced off wooden paddles as many times in a row as they could be hit. We blew soap bubbles from wire rings while Dan and Paul traded marbles with their friends, on the lookout for cat eyes and boulders.

Mama always made a dishpan (not the one we washed dishes in) of potato salad and always a big pot of collard greens. My sister Carzella, who lived up the road, made her to-die-for pound cake and banana pudding. Thad Lampton came out to a couple of Papa's picnics. He was the white bank president. It was Lampton himself who, at one of these picnics, got Papa to tell his story of how he came to be such a successful farmer — by far, in fact, the most successful in the neighboring region.

"Well, for one thing, I was born into it," Papa told Thad Lampton. "Luther and I saw our mother work hard in the fields every day, and we learned from our own father that not every piece of land is worth farming on. Moving to our new homestead was a smart thing to do — we needed richer soil for our cotton, corn, and potatoes, and my father knew where to find it. The old land was full of Bermuda grass and hard as a brick. To till it was near impossible. You could not get fertilizer into it. Those extra acres gave my Pa land for hay, too, for his cows and mules. Meantime, he rented out the old place to a tenant farmer, as I did after that. My Pa's brothers were always there to guide me. Harry, Stephen, Willis — they all knew what they were doing." Papa knew Lampton would mention Uncle Paul, infamous and then famous far and wide. "Paul was the biggest influence," Papa said. He knew Lampton thought he would say just the opposite. Papa continued.

"Uncle Paul was strong as an ox. But that's not the point. For a long time when I was little he reminded me of those ministers who, by necessity, migrate from farm to farm, home to home, bringing the brethren together and at the same time often gravitating to the fullest

45

tables and the most bountiful cooks and the tastiest meals, if you know what I mean. Well, Paul did not work the land like everybody else. And he did not work anything else, either. But somehow he was his own piece of work, floating from brother to brother, who meanwhile floated him loan after loan. Life was a breeze. He was offered work. There was always extra clearing to be done — trash and stumps, wood hauling, hay gathering. But much as Paul liked having money in his pockets, he was never around to earn it or pay it back, not even to his friends."

Old man Lampton wanted to know what he did with it all. "It's a little embarrassing," Papa began, "but if you want to know, I followed him one day. Now this was quite an adventure, at least behind the scenes, for as far as my eye could see — it started at the juke joint. She was pretty enough, they always were, and the piano player pounded out some nice rag, Joplin-style, and they sailed over the dance floor like you never saw before, and soon enough, right into the back room. Well, a few bills fell from his hand as they walked out the back door, and down the street they strolled to the general store. Flour, sugar, vanilla extract, lemon extract all got plopped on the counter, followed by bills from Paul's pocket plus a little extra, and down the road they went to her own parlor, where the pound cake got made, sure enough, if you know what I mean. Yes, Paul was popular with the ladies, and they were popular with him. And in general, he could talk the horns off a billy goat. But when it came to his debtors, one day or another they'd put him in jail — one after another, in one town or another, for the only reason they needed to give — 'he owes us too much money.'"

"Well," said Lampton, fat enough in his own pocketbook, "I'm sure any of your uncles could have bailed him out."

"Of course, and they did, time after time, and there was a next time. Like the time he ended up behind bars in Gulfport down on the coast. Willis and Harry and I paraded down on horseback for sixty miles like the Three Musketeers. My Uncle Harry sold an ox to get Paul out of trouble with a man over his wife. Willis nearly went broke fooling with Paul. You could get bricks and manpower to build a chimney with what you had to pay to bail Paul out twice."

Lampton wanted to know what happened but probably knew all this on his own anyway. Papa continued. "As the story goes, one day it all stopped. The long stay-overs stopped; the loans stopped; the smooth talk stopped; the bail out of jail stopped. Neighbors, friends, brothers, they all stopped. And Uncle Paul, with nowhere else to turn, turned inward. He moved up to Prentiss, got small jobs to start with, cutting lumber, hauling logs, picking cotton, plowing, and any work he could find. Then he got himself a two-ton truck and hauled for other farmers and built barns and fences. He buys a piece of land and gradually a few acres more, and finally he's amassed a hundred acres or more. Paul settled down as a farmer in his own right. That, you had it from your father, and I did from mine, but Paul was living proof of two things: you could squander it all, and you could also start with nothing and make something of yourself. Change is a real possibility."

Chapter 2

Our Own Coloring Book

It is late afternoon, before sundown, and everything around the house is quiet. There's nothing for us to do in the fields. It's springtime and the weather is perfect. The cool months are over and the hot summer months haven't started. Mama's sitting on the front porch in her rocking chair dipping snuff. Papa's in the back field. Jimmy and I are lying on the living room floor, feeling the coolness of the linoleum under us. The Sears Roebuck catalogue fills our dreams as we flip through its pages. At one time or another, we've bought just about everything in it.

I hear Mama talking to somebody out front. We stop and look up to see who. It's Miss Vera, our white neighbor who lives down the road on the other side of the house. She's walking up to the front porch with Joyclyn and Carol, two of her sister's children. We jump up and hurry out to say hi. Miss Vera sits in a rocking chair and starts talking to Mama. Joyclyn and Carol follow Jimmy and me into the living room, walking past the piano and to the catalogue on the floor. Carol takes out a little white candle from her pocket. The only candle we've ever seen was in the Sears Roebuck catalogue. Carol has a match in her pocket. She takes it out, strikes it on the floor, and lights the candle. Then we all sprawl on the floor. We tear pages out of the catalogue and lay the pages close together on the floor. Carol draws the outline of a dog while Jimmy and I watch the wax drip down the sides of the candle. It's a wonder to us, because Mama never uses candles. A few minutes

48

later, Mama comes inside and walks through the living room. She pats me on the head and says, "You pretty little thing." She also pats Joyclyn and Carol and says the same thing. We keep right on playing and never look up. We're five and six years old and don't have a worry in the world.

Other times, we'd go to Miss Vera's house to play. Once one of the older sisters, J'Neal, was courting a boy, and she wrote his name all over her notebook page. She wrote it as many different ways as she could, over and over. She had to be in love.

We had other white friends, Shirley Rose and Charree. I can see their brother, Horace Melvin, roaring down the back gravel road with his girlfriend, Mae, waving and honking the horn at us while we picked cotton. They lived in a log house down the road from old man Harris. It was the only log house in all the neighborhoods.

Our colored playmates lived within walking distance, so we saw them on a regular basis too— home, school, and church. Fannie Mae and Sue, Frances and Helen, and others.

The good old Sears Roebuck catalogue showed us a lot of pictures of children and dolls, all white. They were the only dolls we ever saw. Turning page after page, I wanted one of the little white rubber or plastic dolls. Mama would have us write Santa Claus a letter and tell him what we wanted for Christmas. One time she bought us one of the little dolls from the store in Columbia. We didn't play with it for very long.

Another time, Mama surprised Jimmy, Darlene, and me with a little wooden doll. We were so happy, but we didn't ask for dolls every year. The best year was when Papa built us a big, wooden wagon, one with four wheels and a handle. That wagon pleased us more than anything we'd ever gotten for Christmas. We played with it, in it, on it, pulling each other all over the place. We hauled things in it, everything from pecans off the tree to wood for the fireplace. When part of the wagon broke off, Papa fixed it and we started all over again. We had that wagon long after Christmas and loved it. Having it went past the initial gratification of receiving it on Christmas Day, or getting a stocking full of fruits and nuts, or even the store-bought white dolls. It was a plaything we could use to do everyday chores.

I was never unhappy with what I got at Christmas time. Mama would say, "You all have plenty to eat and a roof over your heads. That's a good enough Christmas." She didn't make too big a deal out of the holiday. She baked fruitcakes and pies and prepared a few sweets to eat but was never big on special presents. When we were little, she used to go out and chop down a small pine tree. She'd carry the tree up to the house and string it with hard red berries she picked out of the woods. They weren't good to eat, but were so shiny and red, they looked pretty. Mama loved hanging strung berries on the Christmas tree.

Shirley Rose, one of my childhood friends, is shown here in her 1954-1955 school portrait.

The night before Christmas, Mama would tell us a story, usually about the reindeer. We couldn't wait to go to bed in order to get up the next morning to see what Santa Claus had brought us. Papa had three or four nails just above the fireplace with stockings hanging down from them. During the night, he and Mama filled them with lots of fruit — apples, oranges, tangerines — and plenty of nuts, including pecans, walnuts, and hickory nuts. The stockings were always full. And when we got up, we ran up to the fireplace and got those big stockings full of goodies.

A Cup of Sugar

One Saturday, Mama was baking a cake and ran out of sugar. She called Jimmy and me into the kitchen, gave Jimmy a small brown paper bag, and sent us over to Miss Harris's house to borrow some. With our little brown bag, we set out walking. Going somewhere was one of the simple joys of childhood, especially for four- and five-year-olds.

As we casually walked down the gravel road, an old Ford pickup drove by, kicking up what felt like a dust bowl. The fact was there was so much to see. Wild buttercups dotted the roadside. In the spring, the dogwoods looked like puffy white clouds, they were so heavy with blossoms. Black-eyed Suzies poked their heads up as if to say "hello." Pastel May pops sprang from vines creeping along the edge of the woods. Their scent was unmistakable. I could always detect a mockingbird when I heard it chattering away like a jay, or a woodpecker boring into the pine bark for bugs. Bushy-tailed squirrels darted around the trunk of an old oak tree, rustling though foliage, chasing each other for fun until they heard my gait from the walking stick I'd found along the roadside. Up the tree they raced, out on a limb to nibble on a nut, gawking at Jimmy and me below.

A cottontail sped through the woods as another truck came roaring down the road with the everlasting honking of the horn and waving of arms. "Howdy, Little Mae and Noah," driver and passenger called out, sending regards to Mama and Papa but gone before we could respond. About halfway to Miss Harris's, a little creek trickled past a blueberry bush and ran alongside or crossed the road if it had rained a lot. The silvery water was so clear you could see tiny black minnows swimming over gray rocks the size of baseballs. Tinder from old tree limbs was carried along by the same gust of wind that floated the sweet scent of honeysuckle to my nostrils. Mama always told us not to dawdle. But there was so much to discover.

Hssss ... Hssss

I stopped. The sound came from the side of the road. Jimmy said it was the breeze, but I had my stick in hand. Once I killed a snake behind the house — a big one, black and mean. I'd spotted it in the small cotton field, but today, there was no such luck finding one.

Miss Harris's big white wooden house stood right there in the fork of the road. The yard was fragrant with green grass and gardenias. Red and gold dahlias framed the house. Deep, wine-colored bearded irises grew along the chain-link fence built after their grandson, "First James," was born. The rainbow of colors was such a delight, but what really caught me was their windmill for pumping water. It set me dreaming. Our mailbox stood next to theirs, a plain tin box on a wooden pole. A letter, a postcard from far away ... what would it say? What news would it bring? What were they eating, driving, and singing, whoever it was, so far away.

We walked right up to the front door and knocked. Coloreds were known to go to the back door of whites in some areas. Not us. Miss Harris came to the door and spoke to me and Jimmy. Her voice was tender and she wore a warm smile. We told her Mama sent us to ask for a cup of sugar, that she's all out and is making a pound cake. Miss Harris led us into the kitchen. She was a tall, white woman, big-boned but with a thin face and pointy features. She wore a long prairie dress with a long apron all the time, and with her graying honey-colored hair pulled back in a bun, she looked like she belonged on a wagon train. Sometimes after spring showers, when we walked by or peered out from the back of our pickup truck as we rode past, we would see Miss Harris out in her boots, raincoat and hat, fixing the fence that kept the cows in. She was strong and could do about anything around the house, which gave her a sense of composure we all admired.

Walking back through her living room where she kept the patch-work quilts folded over the couch like an ever-changing kaleidoscope, we found she had a lot more than one cup of sugar in the bag she handed us. Mama was going to have sugar left over. Miss Harris would do that.

Earldene

Jimmy and I were closest in age, thirteen months apart, and we did more things together. Jimmy was born a twin, a boy named Earldene, who died at the age of six months. My brother Tootsie, who was seventeen at the time, happened to be in the house that morning while Mama was cooking in the kitchen. Mama went up the hall to look in the room where the twins were sleeping and noticed that Earldene seemed quieter than usual. She went over to the bed and pulled the covers all the way back. Earldene's face and arms and legs were still; he appeared to be asleep.

All of a sudden, Mama cried out loud, "Lordy, Noah!" Papa was down the back field, already at work. Mama picked Earldene up and patted him on his back, but he didn't cry. Tootsie stood in the doorway scared, waiting for Mama to tell him what to do. Mama wrapped Earldene in a blanket and set out walking over to Miss Harris's house just down the road. Tootsie was in tow right behind her, while Mama cried in distress. Miss Harris took one look and knew Earldene was dead. She walked Mama back to the house. Tootsie ran and got Papa and they drove downtown to the hospital where the doctor proclaimed Earldene dead. Miss Harris was not just a neighbor; she was a friend to Mama.

It had always been Jimmy who was the sickly one as a baby, not Earldene. I always wondered what he would have grown up to be, what kind of brother he would have been, or if he would have any special talents as Jimmy did. Would he have played basketball or baseball, or laid brick like Dan and Paul? Would he have gone to college with Jimmy? Over the years, all these things would cross my mind at times and I would feel sad for Jimmy and me.

Mama and Papa would let us do a lot of things but not in white folks' houses. We could not clean house, wash clothes, iron clothes, or babysit for whites. It seemed like easy money to us, but we couldn't do it. They'd tell us we had enough things to do around the house. We would go with Mama and Miss Ella when they went over to some white woman's house that was sick and shut in. We would mop floors, wash clothes, and clean up, including sweeping the dirt yard. As part of Mama's home mission work, we did exactly that and more. But not for pay.

Instead, Papa paid us to clean trash, pick quilting cotton for Mama, or perform other menial Saturday morning jobs. We would have spending money. Papa said there's nothing wrong with working in white folks' houses, but he and Mama didn't want us to do it. He and Mama worked hard and made their own way. There was no looking at white folks in awe. If it was farm stuff, wagons or tractors broken down, or something to do with mules, cows, or hogs, Dan, Paul and Papa would help our white neighbors.

Hoy

A little white boy is running around in his parents' yard, playing with everything and anything in sight. There are bricks stacked up all around, big bags of dusty cement mix, wheelbarrows, shovels, hoes, and scaffolds all about. The little boy runs under the scaffolds as his father's voice is heard in the distance to "stay away from there; you could get hurt." He continues to play, for he knows a pickup truck will be coming around the curve real soon.

The engine of the truck is heard down the road. The excitement builds up in the boy. Once the truck arrives, the little boy jumps on the driver's shoulders for his daily ride. They walk around to see what has to be done for the day. Looking at yesterday's progress, Papa is nodding his head up and down; so far he feels satisfied. The little boy holds on tight and he imitates Papa as he looks around and nods his head up and down. He probably feels he's a builder himself. Papa reaches back and grabs him under the arm with one hand to lift him off his back. Hoy, the little boy, laughs all the way down to the ground. This is a memory he recalls today, more than sixty years later.

Integrated Socializing

White men came out to our house, sat on the front porch day and night, and talked to Papa for hours. They went hunting together, men like Old Man Moore and Mr. Kendrick, dressed in overalls, faded blue work shirts, and worn brown shoes who got their shotguns off the rack across the back window of their truck and came up to the porch to chew Prince Albert tobacco and spit out the juice. It would be September and rabbit hunting season. Another time, it might be Old Man Stringer, Mr. McKinney, Herrin, or Lampton, who liked hunting partridge. They all, at some time, came out to hunt with Papa, and with Uncle Shug, who came along for the fun of it. Uncle Artis (Shug, one of Mama's brothers) was like some kind of expert with his twelve-gauge automatic shotgun. When he felt like wasting tobacco or telling lies, he'd call a hunting party together. He'd let go of his gig for the day—the two-wheel, mule-drawn cart he used to deliver the mail between Oloh and Columbia—wave good-bye to his wife, Mattie, top off his flask of whiskey, fill up his pouch with Prince Albert, and be off to collect his brothers, Gilbert (Tobie) and Montes (Sonny), and any white men who thought they were good hunters.

None of them had the gun Uncle Shug had. Theirs had to be reloaded each time they shot it. He'd tilt his head and roll his eyes as he spun his tales 'til there was no way he didn't convince you not to be scared to death. Sebe Dale, Sr., the judge in downtown Columbia, loved sugarcane. He came out to the house many times to get it. His son, Sebe Dale, Jr., only recently retired as a judge in Columbia, Mississippi. He is someone we all continue to know.

They talked about the farm and any problems with their work. They talked about their children, too, especially sons off to war. The white man up the road had a small crop duster plane. He sprayed crops when needed, for colored and white farmers alike. They were the richest white family we knew out here in the country.

Segregation at Its Best — When You're Sick

Later that year, when I was four years old, I got sick. My ears felt so bad that Mama and Papa had to take me to the hospital in downtown Columbia, and I didn't mind one bit if that would make them stop hurting. But the old gray building was ugly, with dingy gray walls that used to be white and long hallways that had tall windows with bars and old, gray, hard floors. My room was in the back of the building and outside the window was an alleyway. The room held four cribs for small children, with rails all around them, like metal. The floor was cold concrete, and there was one big, green swinging door through which to enter the room.

The white nurse gave Mama a dreary old smock to put on me. Mama sat at the head of the bed and crocheted a blue and white doily. There were two other little girls in there who just stared at me. The nurse came back in and gave me my first shot in my butt. I cried and cried. Mama was standing right there and tried to comfort me, and so did the nurse. Finally, she told me I would get some ice cream very soon. When I heard that, I stopped crying. Mama patted me on the back. Every day it was a shot in the butt, and I cried every time. The nurse just dipped that cotton ball into some alcohol and plunged that needle. "Now that didn't hurt so much, did it?" Yes, it did!

The other two girls cried a lot, even if they weren't getting shots. I never saw any white children in the hospital. They went to a different section. Sometimes I would hear people talking or children crying or playing. From the noise, I knew other children were there. The day finally came when I could go home. Mama was already there, as she was every day, and when I got my shot, I didn't cry. I was going home, where I could play and be with Mama and Papa and my sisters and brothers, where I was safe and free.

Another time I had to go to a dentist's office. I remember walking into a room that was cold with a big chair and a lot of gadgets around it. I was really scared. Mama held my hand tight, because I was pulling back. The white doctor came over, scooped me up, and put me down in that big, old, cold chair. Mama was right there, looking like she was on the doctor's side and not mine. I just tried to get out of that chair. Mama held me in while the doctor got something that looked like a mask, all the time saying how it will stop hurting in just a few minutes; all I had to do was wait and see. I was looking up at Mama, all wide-eyed, kicking and screaming, fighting for my dear life. That man, the dentist, put that mask-like thing over my face. I kicked; I just knew he was trying to smother me to death. I was not about to let him do it without a fight. Mama kept telling me to stop and let him do it. In a second, I was out—I don't remember anything else. When I woke up, Mama was telling me that we were going home. The dentist had pulled my tooth, and I felt a big hole in my mouth where the tooth used to be. I was so glad to be going home.

If any of us had a really bad cold or any kind of chest congestion, Mama boiled hot water and soaked a towel in it. Then she squeezed the water out, covered our chests with Vick's VaporRub and put a lot more of the Vick's on a towel. Then she laid the towel over our chests and covered the towel with a half quilt. This would clear up our chests, sinuses, and heads. Mama had to do this from time to time with all of us as we were growing up.

Jimmy would have sore throats more than the rest of us children, and one time she had some kind of fever. When Jimmy was a teenager, Dr. Nicholas, our colored doctor in Columbia, told Papa she had an enlarged heart. He said it was too big and not to let her do hard or heavy work. So Myrtis and I would pull the bigger sacks in the cotton field with Dan and Paul, and Jimmy had a smaller one. Even with housework, we did the heaviest and worst. She would sweep the floors and wash the dishes, but climbing the windmill and milking the cow (we didn't have to milk the cow, I just wanted to) was something she never did. Driving the tractor was totally out of the picture (even for Myrtis), and the car was not to her liking nor were the things I did. A tom-girl like me, she wasn't.

Darlene would take the cake as far as not being a country girl. She told Papa she wasn't supposed to be a farmer. She never got sick, either. Myrtis could do anything, but she didn't milk the cow. Nor did she ever get sick. They never went to the hospital with anything.

Old Man Stringer

There were a few special times when the whites invited the coloreds into their churches. One such occasion was the death of Arthur Stringer. The Improve Baptist Church held a big funeral for him, and Stringer's son, Quinn, invited two colored men to attend, Papa and K.C. Lumzy. Papa had built chimneys for many in the Stringer family, and K.C. Lumzy had known the Stringers for years. Papa was fifteen years younger than Arthur Stringer, and K.C. was just a bit younger than Papa. The honor of being included in his funeral ceremony at the white church was noteworthy.

What Everybody Knows

A man died one night under mysterious circumstances at a local store. It was alleged that he stumbled and fell and hit his head on the corner of the concrete mound between the gas pumps outside. So the story goes. Supposedly one of his sons was there and observed this, but the store owner's son pulled a rifle on him and prevented him from calling for help. He was dead as a doornail when the ambulance made it out from Columbia. Another man had died at the sawmill, "in the middle of work," they said, by somehow falling on the saw. His body was cut almost in half. A few other men from the neighborhood were found stabbed to death.

One night the body of a middle-aged man was found lying by the edge of the road near the schoolhouse. Bruised and lifeless, his arms fallen out of the straps of his torn overalls, he lay in a mess of blood and cracker crumbs. How long he'd been there no one knew, but his breath still smelled of whiskey and fish. Conventional wisdom asked if this was about a can of sardines or something else that had never been paid for. It was one of those unusual deaths in our neighborhood.

The Café

One Saturday, I went to downtown Columbia just to get out. When I got there, I walked right through the front door of the little café on Broad Street. The side door was the entrance for coloreds, leading to the back of the café. When I sat down to order a hamburger and a Coke, the white waitress came right over and asked what I was doing there, telling me I was supposed to be in back. I noticed a few colored people in the back, behind the kitchen. They were all looking at me, wide-eyed. I asked for a hamburger and a Coke, again. She told me to hurry up and threatened to call the police. I told her, "I don't care, I want to eat." The police never came, and the whites just stared. I ate, got up, and left. I don't know if she called the police, or if she didn't because she knew I was Noah's girl, or if she just decided not to bother. I did it again, taking my nephew and niece, Larry and Lynda, with me when they were very young.

I guess it was because I was just plain mad that I wasn't allowed to go through the front door. For the same reason, I stood in the "whites only" line at a hamburger stand, and most of the time the whites in line didn't say a word. They never pushed me out of line. And when I would drink from the "whites only" water fountain, they just looked surprised. The normal "Nigger" was not supposed to be in that line. Yet calling me a "Nigger" was never anything that hurt my feelings. I didn't feel bad about myself for being black; I didn't feel less smart or pretty. Mama and Papa had taken care of what I thought about myself by the time I was big enough to talk and walk. At the time I took the liberties in the "white" line, I was fourteen years old and just not afraid.

I was well aware of segregation, but hostility and hatred of white folks was not a part of my upbringing. The schools, churches, public places, water fountains, hamburger stands all had big labels: "Colored," "Whites." Mama and Papa were directly responsible for how I felt about white folks. It was never if it wasn't for white folks I could do this or that, or be this, or have that. That was not Mama and Papa's way of bringing us up. In school, my teachers never told us not to do something or be something because of white folks. They all attended college and some went to college outside the state. There was never a question of going; it was accepted that we would.

By this time, I often bargained with Papa about going downtown on Saturday afternoons to see friends from our school and other schools, to shop, to walk around, to see and be seen. It was socializing at its best — walking up and down the sidewalks, in and out of stores. It was the thing to do.

Because we worked in the fields every day and until noon on Saturdays, I thought we should be allowed to go downtown on a Saturday afternoon. I also questioned why we had to go to so many church functions. We had our choir practice and Sunday school, and the regular Sunday church service and I didn't think we needed prayer meeting on Wednesday nights on top of it all. I never thought we'd be any better for going, and I told Papa so. (I felt that if I gave Papa a good reason, he would come around. If not, I would just stay mad.) Darlene and Jimmy were standing in the doorway, waiting to hear what Papa had to say. He finally said it was okay for us to go downtown on Saturday afternoons, and he let up on our church activities. "You all can go." We couldn't get dressed fast enough.

In downtown Columbia, which came to be our favorite spot for hanging out, the water fountains were labeled "Colored" or "White," even though they were side by side. There were no indoor bathrooms for us coloreds. If we wanted to use public toilets, we had to go to one outside, located down by the courthouse. We could use the front door and buy anything in any of the stores, but the hamburger stand had separate windows, one labeled "White," and the other "Colored." The little restaurant on Broad Street that we passed as we entered Columbia had a side entrance for coloreds. The picture show had a small upstairs area that required us to use side stairs because we had to sit upstairs in the balcony. Any place where coloreds and whites would be in the same building had totally separate seating and entrances. The Greyhound bus station bathrooms were labeled colored and white.

But there was no walking around with my head down, afraid to look straight at white folks or talk in front of them on the streets; there was no moving to one side when passing them on the sidewalk or being ashamed of my dress or shoes and I walked around downtown. Never was I ashamed of my kinky hair. The land gave us an identity. Work of substance defined us. It taught us what we could do to survive and be independent. It gave me self-confidence and strength, and independence from whites.

When Papa was a twenty-year-old man in 1912, he knew very well the extent to which whites would go to dehumanize colored folks. One Mississippi white senator, who served from 1912 to 1918, aimed his campaign at the small white farmers. Being politically racist and powerful, his policies were contradictory. He was against capital punishment but favored lynching. He felt that to educate Negroes would spoil a good field hand—and would cause them nothing but frustration, because their dreams and expectations could never be realized. Lynching them was proper because they raped white women. Fortunately, all whites did not share his beliefs. Colored folks could go on about their business: to work hard, to get an education, to hold on to their identity and continue to hold on to their souls, their strength, and their ability to survive.

On a given Saturday night, an old colored man might be walking down a back country road enjoying the night. He may or may not have been drinking. When a couple of white men driving down the same road saw him, they'd think nothing of stopping and beating him up. The next day when his family found him, they were too scared to go to the police. Papa said the police would do nothing about it anyway.

Whistle-Stop Town

It's cotton-picking time in the summer of 1955 and all I can think of is going into the tenth grade. I'm fifteen years old, and things are looking up and my prom years are getting closer. But in another part of Mississippi, up in the Delta region of Money, Mississippi, the nation has to face the aftermath of an assault on humanity as heinous and obscene as any violation committed under slavery.

The image of Emmett Till's disfigured face jumps off the page of *Jet* magazine and stays in our minds forever. At his funeral in Chicago, his mother left the casket open for the world to see and young boys and girls to learn from. Mamie Till, top of her class and becoming a schoolteacher, had sent her son down to Money, Mississippi, to visit his father's birthplace. After working in the fields, teenaged Emmett went into a little store, not unlike our Miss Flavor's store up the road from our house, to buy bubblegum. The store was run by whites. With his usual flair, unaware of the life and death rules his mother had tried to teach him about the South, he made the mistake of whistling at a pretty white woman behind the counter as he left the store. For this, he would never go home to Chicago.

The murderers were acquitted, and then they sold the details of their crime to the media. Mamie Till did not succeed when she appealed to President Eisenhower to reopen the case. But she continued to talk about Emmett in the classroom, at PTA meetings, church gatherings, and at many other organizations that gave weight to what would later be called the "Civil Rights Movement." What would our history books make of this atrocity? What would they teach us about our courts, our laws, our unspoken truths, and our history? The civil rights of black America — unprotected by law to this day.

The Vote

There were things going on bigger than us in our community that many country folks may not have known about. Up in Jackson, Mississippi, a hundred miles north, a war was going on between Theodore Bilbo, a U.S. senator from Mississippi, and black America. In December 1946, he campaigned furiously against blacks voting in the Democratic primary. He blasted the war service of black soldiers.

Mama's brother-in-law, Uncle T.B. Wilson, and many veterans testified against the senator. Uncle T.B. dressed up in his blue suit, white shirt with tie, his head gray and balding with age and wisdom. Being the teacher that he was, he greeted half the people in the courtroom person by person, with endless nods and smiles. He was ready, he said, to scoop up his testimony as if it was a hundred-pound sack of the knowledge of life. An awesome silence hovered over the room as Thurgood Marshall took a seat, the weight of legitimate authority settling like an ominous cloud.

Uncle T.B. was the first to take the stand. He sounded like a lawyer and wore many hats. A college graduate, a schoolteacher in Columbia; a principal in Jackson schools for thirty years; a real estate agent; founder and president of the Progressive Voters' League, member of the Jackson NAACP and the Negro Chamber of Congress. Uncle T.B. was the first Negro to vote in Mississippi and instrumental in getting the Negro citizens of Mississippi to vote in large numbers at the primaries.

The fact that he raised his children entirely on his own after his wife, Julia Dukes, died when they were very young, remained little mentioned in his public history but was held in awe by the Exposé and Dukes families. But due to their father's activism, his daughters hung quilts over the windows of their family home to guard against bricks flying through the glass. His daughter Gladys, alive today, says they were so afraid they would gather into one room, with only one light on.

My first cousin, one of Uncle T.B.'s daughters, gave me a copy of the original *Clarion Ledger* newspaper article: Jackson, Mississippi, Tuesday morning, December 3, 1946. Also, the December 16, 1946, issue of *Life* magazine ran an article of the Bilbo hearing. A copy of the mural on the wall behind Uncle T.B.'s head as he testified hangs in the old Federal Court House in Jackson, Mississippi.

Many veterans and men throughout Mississippi testified about the problems they had trying to register to vote and the negative effects their efforts had on them and their families. It was some scary times. The ability of black Americans today to vote and create change in communities, schools and churches locally as well as nationally was made possible by brave and determined people years before you or me. It's important that we never forget how our freedoms came about and the effect inequality had on every aspect of our lives. Today there is no cost for voting. No one stands in your way at the polls. All you have to do is register. No testing, no fear, no threats.

I was frightened when Papa talked about how Uncle T.B. and his children might be beaten up, put in jail, even killed. At the same time, Papa told us not to worry, that he didn't believe the old white racist men would go so far as to kill any Negro for trying to vote. But they would do everything to break you down, especially emotionally — to break your spirit and try to take your soul. If they succeeded in doing that, a colored person didn't stand a chance.

Papa reminded us of how slave owners couldn't break the will — the spirit and the determination — of the slaves. Grandpa Daniel was adamant about not letting anyone try to make you feel less than you are. Papa said that's what he was taught to believe and what he felt as a child. There were men that Papa talked about. One in particular was the president of Howard University, in Washington, D.C., the biggest Negro college in the country. His name was Mordecai Johnson. Papa said he was the smartest man he ever read about. Mr. Johnson was a minister and spoke out about the "Jim Crow" churches. He also traveled all over the South, studying the conditions of colored schools and colleges.

Papa learned from his father, Grandpa Daniel, and Grandma, and his uncles, the farmers, to help people when he could. He saw what he could do that would help them in the best way, and that was to have food to eat, out of his "special field" years later and giving a lot of people work in the cotton fields.

During the 1940s, there was a lot of social hostility across the country. Colored soldiers were beginning to demand their rights at home, the same rights they had fought overseas to preserve. The South fought back by killing colored war veterans. At that time, a man named Walter White, president of the NAACP, told President Truman what was going on with Negro veterans. Truman signed a bill by the President's Committee on Civil Rights that included legislation regarding lynching, segregation, poll taxes, voting rights, and equal employment. In 1948, the law was passed to outlaw segregation in the armed services.

Papa and my older brothers served in the segregated armed forces. A Negro soldier could fight and be killed in a war for his country without enjoying the rights of the country that he fought for. During his first few years in Washington, the late congressman Charles Diggs was assigned to the House Committee on Veterans' Affairs. As an enlisted man and officer during World War II, he was well acquainted with the policies of segregation and discrimination in the U.S. Armed Forces. He was motivated to change the nation's policies. In 1959, President Eisenhower sent Diggs on a fact-finding mission, principally in the Pacific Air Forces (PAC-AF) command from Hawaii to the Philippines, plus other Pacific islands and Japan. Diggs was to report back on the conditions of minorities in these areas of the U.S. Armed Forces. The first Negro four-star Air Force general, Lt. Colonel "Chappie" James, accompanied him. They had both been stationed at the Black American Army Airfield Headquarters in Tuskegee, Alabama.

Congressman Diggs' comprehensive report, supported by extensive interviews and on-site investigations, initiated the creation of an Armed Force Commission to address segregation and discrimination within our command. This commission was continued in 1961 under the next president, John F. Kennedy, whom Congressman Diggs had supported in the 1960 general election. Thus, Diggs was acknowledged as the catalyst for improved race relations in the Armed Forces, at a pace that made laws and changed laws and names of committees that dealt with segregation and discrimination within its own armed forces, which is a service that protects the whole United States of America. Will there ever be real justice?

The Bonus March: Promises, Promises

Papa remembered well the "Bonus March" on Washington in 1932, just as he remembered the hard times the country was going through. Country folks and city folks alike were struggling to survive. The depression of the 1930s that no one saw coming led to soup lines in cities all over the country. Farmers with little to no land of their own struggled to feed their families.

World War I veterans throughout the country were not only unhappy but angry as well because of promises from the government for their war efforts. This money would be in certificates that would mature in twenty years, a trust fund of about one thousand dollars. The veterans that went overseas got a little more. Negro soldiers hadn't been allowed to go overseas because they were not trusted to bear arms. A thousand dollars was a lot of money back then; it could feed and house a family for six months.

During the depression, men were out of work for so long they began asking for their money. The House of Representatives passed the bill and people got excited, but the Senate voted it down and President Hoover vetoed it. Riots broke out across the country, and hunger marches and unemployment protests ended up on the grounds of the White House. Veterans with their families boarded trains all over the country for Washington, D.C. Camps were set up, clapboard shelters and makeshift commissaries. Two veterans were killed in the riots, women and children were gassed, camps were burned, fires broke out, and terror reigned everywhere. The president sent in troops to restore order. They used machine guns and tanks, while the veterans were armed with bricks. War was waged by a government upon its own veterans.

Papa served in the army from June 18, 1918, to March 24, 1919, and left Grandma and Grandpa Daniel Exposé's farm. After his discharge, he was fortunate to return home to his parents and to start his own farm. He was able to make a living and support his new wife, unlike many veterans during the Depression years. The special field he provided across the road became even more important because of the times and the economic conditions of so many.

By 1943, there was another world war, and my brothers enlisted in the armed services to fight overseas.

Chapter 3

Brothers and Sisters

My Brothers Came Marching Home

Growing up in a big family is an adventure — a continuous series of events, situations and happenings. With so many brothers and sisters, we were divided into age-related groups to keep us straight. In my family, there were the first four boys; the next two girls; and the last six of us who grew up together — two boys and four girls.

My oldest brother is 21 years older than I, and the fourth oldest is 14 years older. There was no way I knew who they were when they came home. My first memory of them was when I was three years old. It wasn't until I was six that I began to see differences and similarities in my siblings. Some I liked, some I didn't, others were not decided on immediately.

Other colored families in our community had up to seventeen children — eleven girls and six boys in one, eight boys and eight girls in another. In every class was a classmate or two from such families. When the sons went off to war, every family worried about them coming home shot up, shell shocked, legs cut off, or not coming home at all. Our white neighbors worried about the same thing. Papa certainly knew the parents of the white boys in the communities. Many an early evening, some old white man would be sitting on the front porch talking to Papa. The war was on everybody's mind — all they talked about.

My six brothers served in the Army and Navy, and the oldest three went overseas in World War II. Papa was in World War I, but served in the United States only.

Furlough: Pleased to Meet You

The photographer runs around like a Cheshire cat and sets up things, making a lot of noise. At the same time, he's shushing us and telling us to be quiet. We are all there. He places three chairs together in front for Papa, Mama (holding Darlene) and Loretta to sit in; the rest of us stand — the youngest up to the oldest, the tallest in back. It's hot, and I want to go outside. Papa holds my hand over the arm of his chair to keep me in. That photographer is s-l-o-o-w. It's fall of 1942, wartime, and my older brothers are home together for the first time. The three oldest — Noah, Jr., Luther, and Clifford — are on furlough. This is the one and only family photo of all of us together.

It was evening and a little cool outside. A fire was going in the fireplace. Mama was dipping snuff and spitting juice into the fire. Papa was chewing tobacco and spitting into his empty red Prince Albert tobacco can sitting on the floor by his rocking chair. The knock on the door was loud and hard; we hadn't noticed the bright car lights, but we'd heard the car. "One of you go see who's on the front porch," Papa said. I got up and took the lamp. When I opened the front door, there stood a man in an army uniform. It was Boy Noah, the oldest, come home. We closed the door and gathered 'round him. Another loud knock and Luther (Tootsie) stood outside. The last knock, loudest of all, was Clifford, home on furlough, laughing.

Mama started crying — going from one to the other, wiping her eyes, not knowing which way to turn. Papa stopped spitting his tobacco juice, eyes wide, grinning from ear to ear, shaking his head, and hugging each one of them. I looked up at these tall men, not knowing who they were until Mama and Papa told us they were our older brothers. I didn't remember ever seeing them before. Each one of them walked

My brothers came marching home in 1942: (left to right) Noah Jr., the serious one; Luther (Tootsie), the historian; Clifford, the military man; Bufford, the laid back brother.

around the room, pulled my chin up, asked me my name. They did the same with Jimmy, Myrtis, and Darlene, who was the baby. They said we looked alike and told Mama and Papa we were pretty little girls. It was a good feeling seeing those brothers all grown up and in uniform, talking to Mama and Papa about people in other countries and how they lived, how they spoke, what they ate, how they looked.

Three years later, in 1945, when I was six years old, Uncle Luther was sitting on the front porch talking to Papa about Boy Noah, Jr., and the war—how all the boys were coming back home, every one of them. "Them Japs not going to kill our boys, not our soldiers. But the bombing was the worst. It had never been that bad before." When Uncle Luther left, I went out on the front porch and asked Papa if the Japs were coming across the water to kill us. "The army will stop them," he said. "They will always stop them. We don't have to worry." I felt so relieved after that and was not scared anymore. I didn't feel my brothers would get killed, and Clifford served for many more years and managed to come home alive and well.

As I got a little older, I began to have some feelings about them from all of Mama's and Papa's talk about what they were like as young boys, the things they did, how they helped Mama and Papa on the farm, their schooling. It made me feel good in my everyday life. They became heroes to me. I bragged about them in school. And I felt I could do anything and nothing would happen to me.

Noah, Jr.

Noah, Jr., the oldest, was born on September 25, 1918. He was inducted into the army and served in direct combat in China and Japan in 1943 for two years and seven months with the China-Burma-India Theater (the CBI), a general geographic reference designating the intersection of East Asia, Southeast Asia, and South Asia as regions linked in the struggle against Japan. But CBI also loosely referred to the military commands of various nations that existed within this geographic region, and for a time it was the name of a specific American military command structure that initially came from the Arcadia Conference held in Washington in December 1941, when Churchill and Roosevelt agreed to a joint command for Southeast Asia. During his term, Boy Noah also worked on the Burma Road. When he came home on furlough, he did a lot of sleeping, eating, and whiskey drinking. He suffered malaria in Burma before returning home, but he recovered.

He was the only one of my four older brothers who came back home to live after the war. He was also the only one to actually live with us in the house. My earliest memories of him are of his spending a lot of time in his room. He slept in the back bedroom across from the dining room, but rarely did he ever sit at our table during meals. Sometimes he would get up and come into the kitchen and get some food from one or two of Mama's pots, but he would take it back into his room to eat it.

By the time I was six or seven, I could smell the whiskey on his breath if he came into the kitchen. We had an icebox then, and once every week or so the ice man came through, down all those country roads, with blocks of ice and a big ice pick on the back of his truck. Milk, butter, and meat didn't seem to spoil back then. The ice man's old, beat-up pickup truck had a faded-out blue cab. I could hear its noisy engine long before it got up to the house. The ice man honked his horn, a horn that reminded me of a broken whistle. He was an old colored man who wore overalls with a blue denim shirt under the bib.

He had a fat belly and laughed a lot. Papa always bought one block of ice and then took his own big pick and broke off big chunks that he put in the upper section of our old icebox to keep everything cold. The remainder of the block was covered with a burlap sack and a small half-quilt. It kept for a few days in the corner of the little storage room off the kitchen.

Many times when Boy Noah had been drinking, he would get up, get a chunk of ice, crush it up, wrap it in a towel, and put it on his forehead. Sometimes he would call out to one of us to bring him some ice for his head. Often, he marched around with a big stick over his shoulder as if it were a gun, and when he did this, he spoke in Chinese. "Wan-dan-leh," he jeered (the game is over). "Tao, kwai-tao! Tao, kwai-tao!" (Run, run away fast.) I didn't like Boy Noah because he acted like he was the boss around the house. And so many times, Papa had to tell him to go back to his room and that he was not going to tolerate any shouting and cursing.

I wasn't scared of Boy Noah, but I sure wished Mama and Papa would do something with him. I didn't know what, but something. For a long time, I would get Papa's rifle, go out in the back field nearby, line up some tin cans, and see how many of them I could hit in the center. I really liked shooting the rifle. Maybe it gave me a feeling of a little extra power, knowing I could use it.

During the times when Boy Noah got out of control, Papa would take him up to Jackson to some veterans' facility, Whitfield, the state hospital, where they told Papa that Boy Noah was "shell shocked" due to the war. Shell shock was described back then as a psychological effect the war had on some soldiers after fighting, killing, seeing all those dead bodies—the whole way of life during war. There would be many of those trips over the years, especially throughout my teenage years— all of them the same—when Boy Noah "went crazy." Mama and Papa could not handle him, so off to Jackson he would go. He would be there for months at a time, his face filled with sad puzzlement. Boy Noah's high, sculpted cheeks fell to hollow, sunken jaws. His thin lips were pursed in doubt, his brows knit in a frown with crevices above them etched with anger, his eyes filled with alarm and worry.

Everything around the house, when he wasn't there, was peaceful and quiet and calm. Whenever he was at home, he didn't socialize with the rest of the family. If I went into the kitchen where he sat by the fire alone and I said something to him, he would respond with a "yes" or a "no." Occasionally he would say one or two words.

Luther

My next-oldest brother, Luther ("Tootsie"), was named after Papa's brother, Luther, and was born on March 14, 1921, and died January 7, 2010. He was inducted into the army with the 392nd Engineer Regiment, which landed in Normandy on June 6, 1944, D-Day. Germany had taken over France, Poland, and Denmark. Later, he was with the European Theater of Operations in England, France, and Germany for two years, one month.

One night in France a truck came upon the place where they were camped out. The driver needed help with problems he was having with the truck. When he got out and walked toward a group of soldiers sitting around, Tootsie stared at him. When the driver walked closer, he and Tootsie broke out into the biggest laughter. It was Pete, a white boy Tootsie went swimming with in a swim hole in the backwoods of Mississippi. The surprise of running into each other in France of all places would be a topic of conversation for years to come.

Tootsie was in direct combat and received five campaign stars: Normandy, Northern France, Rhineland, Ardennes, and Central Europe. Years later, I tried talking with him about the war. It didn't happen. He really had little to say — only where he was, how long he was there, and that it was war. But he did talk about the army and segregation. He said that the only whites with whom he came into direct contact were the officers of their company. The Negro officers ranked over the Negro soldiers. The army set up an agreement with the local town officers that the soldiers, Negro and white, could meet at a local dance hall in South Central England once a week on weekends to socialize and party. All the soldiers met there, two or three regiments at a time. Tootsie said that at first, there was no trouble between them, but after a few weekends, a fight would break out that drew in the whole dance hall.

Someone would start a scuffle on the dance floor, and then it spread all over the floor. Someone on the stage would jump down into the soldiers. The music would carry on half-heartedly, but some of the band members would join the fighting. Tootsie was sure all that fighting was because most of the female entertainment showed more interest in the Negro soldiers than in their white army friends and because of segregation. The Negro soldiers and the whites trained separately and fought in separate lines. They all moved in the same direction, but in separate groups. When the men on the front lines got all shot up and injured and tired, they made their way to the back lines to rest and the Negro soldiers went forward to the front lines. They saw all the whites then.

Tootsie told me that in Japan, the Japanese soldiers saved their necks. When the Japanese came face to face with Negro soldiers, the enemy said, "We no fight you!" That made the white officers mad as hell. When I asked how he got his stars in France, he said it was the "damned war."

After Tootsie was discharged, he returned home for only a few months. He left and went to Tuskegee Institute for six months, and then to Birmingham to attend business school for eighteen months and to study advanced accounting for twelve months. He earned a certificate in business administration, but he said there were very few jobs available at that time, so he started work in the steel mills and made $100 per week, which was, he said, a lot of money. Many servicemen did the same thing, along with boys just out of high school. Funeral homes and insurance companies paid only $50 per week. The steel mill was the place to work in Birmingham. He lived there from 1946 to 1961.

I think Tootsie regretted that he didn't finish school in Tuskegee, because he said it was all his fault that he didn't and that a childhood friend who lived right up the road, one of the Lees, finished at Tuskegee. Tootsie admired him for it.

A big grin covered Tootsie's face as he talked about visits down to Grandpa Emanuel's house. Grandpa Emanuel was known as "Uncle Man" by everybody all over our community and everywhere he traveled. Because he was so well known, people would always blow the horns on their pickup trucks and wave at Grandpa as they roared down the old gravel road. They called out, "Hey, Uncle Man!" Grandpa would wave back and ask Tootsie, "Who was that?" (Grandpa was going blind by then.) Tootsie said he was jealous of him for all the people who knew him, although he himself was only a young boy at the time. Often, Tootsie, Boy Noah, and Clifford went down to Grandpa's just to visit, other times to do chores around the house.

When Grandpa had to use the toilet, Tootsie and Boy Noah, one on either side, each holding a hand, led him down the tall back steps of the house, Grandpa leaning backwards to keep from falling. Tootsie and Boy Noah had to hold on tight. They had six or seven steps to walk down, and with each step, Tootsie would count, "Number one, Grandpa, number two, three ..." until they got down to the ground. Finally, they made it.

Sometimes, Papa went out to pick up Grandpa, or Uncle Shug would drive him out to our house to visit. Grandpa liked to sit on the front porch to listen to the cars and pickup trucks flying down that country road. He listened to the wind, the birds, and the boys playing. One day, Boy Noah was spreading fertilizer in the field across the road in front of the house. Grandpa called out, "Hey, Boy, Whatcha doin'?" "Strewin' cow shit, Grandpa, strewin' cow shit."

Another time, Grandpa was sitting out in a chair in the shade at the field's edge and Tootsie was hanging his plow on the wrong side of the row, on his way back to the end, where he would start over. Grandpa knew what Tootsie was doing and called out, "You're on the wrong side of the row with your plow!"

"How do you know that, Grandpa?" asked Tootsie.

"I can tell by the sound of the plow!" Grandpa told him.

Tootsie was undone. How could Grandpa know so much by the sound of things? "We can't fool Grandpa," he told Clifford. "We can't fool him at all."

Other times, Grandpa just sat on the front porch in a rocking chair and asked one of them to comb his hair. Grandpa's hair was soft and as white as snow.

Tootsie told me good stories about Grandpa Daniel, Papa's pa. How Daniel would fight in a minute. He always walked around with a cane. He wasn't crippled; he thought it was sporty. At church one Sunday, one of the neighborhood drunks was shouting, cursing, and spewing out his guts. Grandpa marched into the churchyard and cracked the man right over the head with his cane. They got into a scuffle. Grandpa's brother, Willis, was in the pulpit preaching and said, "You all wait a minute." His nephew saw what was going on, and he ran over to where a crowd had gathered and jumped into the middle of it. He pulled out a pistol and barked, "Don't nobody move!" One sister fainted on the spot and hit the ground. The crowd scattered in no time. Some ran into the church, some took cover behind parked cars and trucks, and some jumped inside the cars and trucks until the fight was over. Grandpa and Uncle Willis acted like they'd been sipping mint juleps at the Kentucky Derby after it all stopped.

Tootsie told me about the field across the road during the depression and how many families had a hard time. No money to buy gas, cars propped up on blocks in the yard. Some families' crops didn't do well. Colored and whites struggling to survive digging in the earth for food from gardens that were barren.

Sitting around talking to Tootsie on one of his visits, he was reminiscing how as little boys he and Clifford would go places with Mama when Papa wasn't there — one on either side of her, holding her hand. He talked about how pretty she was. Tootsie also said that as a young boy, he drove Grandma fifteen miles to Mt. Bethel and Harmony

Church to organize women for the Home Mission Society, a charitable religious organization serving the needs of the sick and shut-ins. She organized whole districts, such as East Pearl River. Tootsie dropped her off at the church, and she sat on the steps until the women heard from passersby that she was there. She'd tell Tootsie, "You go on back. I'll be all right. I have sandwiches and water. You come back in three days and pick me up." "Okay, Grandma," he'd say. "I'll be back to get you," and he left. But when he came back, Grandma was still sitting on the steps.

"Grandma, didn't the women come out? Where did you sleep?"

"Two came, but that's good. They'll tell the other women in their church, so it was a good trip."

Tootsie just shook his head in sadness that only two women came out.

When I asked him to tell me what it was like when they were young boys growing up, Tootsie shared with me their little trips with Papa. He took Tootsie, my other brothers, and a couple of their friends up to the zoo in Jackson, Mississippi. They also went on fishing and hunting trips. When Tootsie was fourteen and Boy Noah seventeen, Papa took them down to New Orleans and bought them a 1936 Ford because Papa was tired of them borrowing his car on the weekends and staying out late. At that time, there were very few white boys who had a car, much less colored boys. Tootsie and his friends had school during the week, played basketball and softball, went swimming in the nearby offshoot of the Pearl River, and went to house parties on Friday nights.

Another time, when Tootsie and Boy Noah were out with their girls on a Friday night, Boy had an altercation in the backseat with his girlfriend. Boy hit her on the leg with a tire iron. "Ohhhh!" she screamed. "I'm telling the police!" They arrived downtown. "Stop the car," she demanded, and got out and limped to the police station. With her report, the police came right over, grabbed Boy Noah, and put him in jail. Up on the north end of town, in the segregated section of Columbia, there was a colored nightclub owned by a man named John Bridges.

Tootsie drove up there, told Bridges what had happened, and went back downtown to the jail. John Bridges got Boy Noah out of jail. It cost him ten dollars. Papa would have to find out about that from someone else.

Clifford

Clifford, the number three son, born June 27, 1923, was inducted into the navy and served from November 23, 1943, to December 18, 1945. He was stationed in the South Pacific. After two years he came home, went to work in the steel mills in Alabama for three or four years, and, in 1948, enlisted in the army, serving in Germany and Korea. At the same time, you could sign up for two years and get three, or for three years and get four. He served in Korea and Germany in direct combat, making sergeant 1st class. Clifford would talk only to Papa and Mr. Ado Lee (who lived up the road) about the war — never to us children. He retired from the army after twenty years.

I remember when I was a child of about ten or eleven. We were awakened in the middle of the night by a taxi driver knocking on the front door. Papa got up fast because it was so late. As Papa opened the door, bright lights were shining on the front porch, and the white man stood there and said, "I have your son in the car, and he needs some help to get out." But Clifford woke right up, stumbled a little, and marched up the walkway past Papa and the driver, right into the house.

Mama was standing in the doorway. "Oh, Lord, it's Clifford!" He hugged Mama and went straight to the back bedroom and plopped down and went to sleep on the bed. All four of us girls were standing in the living room doorway peeping at Clifford with the biggest grins on our faces, so glad he was home. Dan and Paul were up by now and out on the front porch to see what was going on. The taxi driver was trying to get a big metal suitcase out of the trunk of his car. Dan and Paul helped.

Papa asked the driver how much the fare was. The driver said it was already paid, that they (including the other passenger, a white soldier asleep in the backseat) had paid it in full when they left Jackson, Mississippi. The white soldier lived in Hattiesburg, Mississippi, and the driver told Papa he was on his way to drop off the last one for the night. They were sober enough to give directions, pay the driver, and tell him they had just left Korea. Clifford slept for two days. And about two days later, that same white soldier was sitting on our front porch talking to Papa and getting his share of whiskey out of that metal suitcase, all tied up with a rope. We already knew what was in it because Dan and Paul had opened it, and we couldn't stop laughing.

Clifford had a vivid imagination. He continually found himself getting into all sorts of devilment — everything from chasing cats that were chasing rats to falling out of trees. His imagination was so good that he could read as soon as he could talk, which was by age two. At least this is what Mama thought, until she realized he was making up his own story as he turned each page looking at the pictures. Mama had to start all over again to teach Clifford to read and count before he started school. As an old soldier, he knew all about the wars, way back to the Civil War. He could talk for hours; giving details of what the Americans were doing there, who their leaders were, and what they were like — and, more important, where they went. I don't remember Papa or Mama fussing with my brothers about their drinking.

Once, Clifford and Bufford were in the kitchen and Clifford heard the cat running through the house. When he saw what was going on, he decided to catch it. The cat ran from Mama's and Papa's room, leapt onto the buffet, and jumped up toward the corner of the dining room ceiling and into the loft. Clifford used a chair to climb over the buffet and pulled himself up into the loft. He set out to catch the cat, jumping from beam to beam.

"You better come down there before you fall!" shouted Bufford.

"Because Mama's gonna get you. And you know you can't catch that cat."

"Yes, I can," Clifford yelled down. "I see that old cat. I caught him once before."

Clifford just laughed. Bufford sat there, shaking his head in amazement. Then he heard a crash and saw Clifford fall between the beams, barely catching himself. He swung there by his hands, crying out, "Go get Mr. Ado's boy — get me down!"

"Okay," answered Bufford, but let Clifford hang there for ten or fifteen minutes before he returned with one of the boys and got him down. "I told you that you couldn't catch that cat," he said.

Every chance they got, the boys shot marbles and ran to the store to buy different colored ones. Their other favorite pastime was to fool around with Papa's tools and carpentry equipment that he kept in the car shed. Once, when Clifford and Tootsie were playing with one of Papa's hammers, Clifford wanted to take it away from him. He kept begging Tootsie for it, and finally, Tootsie got tired of listening to him whine, so he just threw it at Clifford when he wasn't looking. The hammer hit Clifford on the jaw and put a hole on it. When he took a breath, air and blood came gushing through that hole. He let out a scream.

"Oh! Clifford, you should have been looking, and not begging so much!" Tootsie said. Clifford just stood there with blood streaming down his face. "I didn't mean to hit you," Tootsie said, and ran up to the house to get Mama. When she came out to the back porch and saw Clifford bleeding, she picked up the tail end of her apron and wiped off the blood. Then she could see how deep the gash was. She wet a clean dish towel with cold water and made Tootsie hold it over the wound. Within a few minutes, she made up some kind of concoction. Tootsie said it was a pasty mixture, like a salve. Mama spread it all over Clifford's jaw, which soon stopped bleeding. Every day Mama applied more of her special salve, until Clifford's jaw healed. Papa gave both Clifford and Tootsie a real good talking to that night about playing with his tools and being so careless. All Tootsie could say was, "I didn't mean to hit him."

Bufford

My brother Bufford was cool before there was cool and laid back before those terms were ever invented. He was the youngest of the four older brothers, born August 8, 1925. Bufford was in the army only a few months before the war ended. It was just luck, because he was drafted back into the army in 1950 and served two years. He was a little more relaxed about his army experience than his three older brothers, but he didn't talk about it specifically. Bufford returned from the army in 1953 and lived in San Francisco, Detroit, and Chicago before returning home to Mississippi in 1967.

When he was only six years old, he was sent up to Grandma and Grandpa's house to live for what turned out to be ten years. They needed someone in the house to help with the chores. Bufford wanted to go, but he also wanted to stay home with his brothers. He missed out on some of the day-to-day life at home, but Papa included him in all the boys' other activities, because he came down to the house every day. When it was getting dark, Mama would say, "Bufford, it's time to go home now." "But I am home," he'd say, and saunter slowly out the door. As it turned out, one or another of the last eight of us would stay up at Grandpa's and Grandma's from a few to many years at a time. Bufford was the first, then Paul followed him, from 1949 to 1950, then Jimmy from 1951 to 1953, of the last four of us. Grandpa's land was left to Bufford, so all the schoolhouse property became his.

Bufford was relaxed all the time. He never got in a hurry or rushed to do anything. He could tell a good joke and poke fun. Laughter came easily to him and he'd tell you in a minute how you had to dress better than that if you were going out with him. My brothers were all rough-housers, and playful.

Girl Talk

Sometimes in the early morning hours, when Papa had to go somewhere, either to work or downtown, his old Ford would not start right
up. So he'd call Carzella and Loretta and they would push the truck all
the way up to the top of the hill on the road right alongside the barn.
That way, when Papa came out to leave, all he'd have to do was jump
inside. Then my sisters would push it off down the hill, which was
steep enough so that the old car's engine started up every time with
such a good jump. Papa would go roaring down the hill and Carzella
and Loretta would stand there and listen until they couldn't hear him
anymore. Meanwhile, Mama was always cooking, it seemed — three
meals a day, every day. When the girls got big enough, they helped out
a lot.

Loretta and Carzella played a lot of games, both at home and at
school. One they played at home was hopscotch, because it could even
be played alone. There were at least three versions played at the time,
each with its own pattern drawn on the ground. Another game involv-
ing fifteen children within a circle at one time was a favorite. Two children were positioned outside the circle with a big ball. They were to
throw the ball into the circle and hit each child until they were all hit
and the game was over. Each child would dodge the ball for as long as
possible. It was a fun game to play because you had to move fast in
order to dodge the ball and keep from colliding with the other children.

In the fields, my sisters picked up the scrap cotton that Mama
used to stuff quilts. They also picked cotton, scrap corn, cucumbers,
and potatoes. They did whatever odd chores needed to be done. Of
course, going to church was routine, going to Sunday school and to
prayer meetings on Wednesday nights. These events structured the week
beyond school, housework, and field work.

To the left of the fence along our barnyard and behind it following
the gravel road was a pasture with a big, steep, sloping hill that ran

down to the creek, crossed by a wooden bridge. There were catfish, perch, and other game fish in the creek. Beyond the creek was the rest of the pasture, which led to the big fish pond and the surrounding area where Papa held a huge picnic every few years.

That hill was so wide and steep from the fence to the creek that every chance Carzella and Loretta got they would go out to the barn, get a burlap sack, and slide down that hill all the way to the creek. Lucille and Ellouise, friends of theirs, would visit, and all of them went out to that pasture to slide down that hill. When they came back up to the house, Mama always knew what they had been doing because the seats of their dresses would be totally covered with a ground layer of dirt.

"I told you girls not to slide down that hill," reprimanded Mama. "All you do is get your clothes dirty, and you could hurt yourselves." "Yes'um, Mama," they'd answer, but every chance they got, off to the pasture they went. The soil there was a light clay color compared to that of the rest of the pasture and fields. The pasture directly alongside the hill ran behind the barn and also down into the side of the back field. The cows were let out of the barnyard and into this back pasture where they were allowed to graze, all the way down to the old gravel pit. The fence around the gravel pit prevented the cows from walking into it. The same gravel pit was where Clifford, Luther, Boy Noah, and Bufford learned to swim. Mama didn't want us— Myrtis, Jimmy, and me — going near that gravel pit.

Loretta

My first memories of Loretta are of her coming home from school to visit us. I was four years old when she left, so it was a few years until I knew who she was. Papa had sent her to Tougaloo College High School in Jackson in 1943 to attend the tenth through twelfth grades. She went on to college from there. Of course, she would get a better education at Tougaloo, but another reason Papa sent her there was to get her away from one of the local boys.

Loretta lived on campus in the dormitory, so her visits were longer during the summers, although she came home on many weekends during the school year, brimming with tales to tell. Setting the pace for the rest of us, she was on the basketball team, sang in the choir, and played the piano. And because she was very talkative, friendly and likeable, she was very popular. Loretta sometimes brought one of her classmates with her when she came to visit for the weekend. Often, it was Sally.

"Sally who?" we asked our big sister. "Where did she grow up? Did they have animals on their farm? Did she pick cotton? Can she drive a car? Does she have any brothers? Can they dance?" Now Loretta couldn't keep up with us! Sally looked like a white girl to us. We were only eight and nine years old and didn't know that whites also went to Tougaloo. Sally was thin, a little tall, and had brown hair. She was friendly and seemed to really enjoy coming down to our house. We liked showing her the barnyard — the chickens, the mules, the pigs, and the hay loft — and walking down to the fish pond.

Once, Loretta brought one of her professors home. He was from Nigeria, wore a suit and tie, had a British accent, and spoke the King's English. He never just answered in a simple phrase or sentence but told a whole story — about tribal elders or sacred trees, spiders that could think, or monkeys who played tricks. He was full of fables and riddles and legends. We loved to hear how in Nigeria, and throughout West Africa, country people raised livestock and village people made water pots from red clay. Their houses were even made of mud. All Darlene and I could think of was the rain melting them to mush. In Nigeria, they had antelopes, bush cows, and elephants. The whole population was Negro, and they spoke in many different dialects.

This professor friend liked walking down by the fish pond and in the back fields with Loretta, and they seemed to do it every chance they got. But he said the garden was what he loved most because they could not grow food in his homeland as easily as Mama had made it seem in ours. The Nigerian soil was less fertile, and also it got very hot, up to a hundred degrees, in the north of Nigeria where he lived. Darlene and I followed only a few steps behind the professor and Loretta on most of their walks. He slept up at Uncle Luther's house and spent the days with Loretta down at our house. I think he wanted to marry our sister, but she thought he was too serious.

Every time she came home to visit, no matter how elegant a suitor she had, Papa ended up giving her money before she returned to school or college. Always, like clock-work, she seemed to run out. One story Loretta told was of Aunt Gladys, Mama's sister,

My sister, Loretta, pictured in 1942, was leaving home for Tougaloo to finish high school.

sending her some store-bought sheets and pillowcases when she went to college at Tougaloo. This made her feel good and special. Loretta was used to the sheets being hand-made from flour sacks that had been boiled and bleached to death until they were snow white. Mama embroidered pretty designs across the borders of the sheets and cases, but to Loretta, store-bought sheets were something else.

For a few years after college, Loretta taught English downtown at the colored high school in Columbia, Mississippi. I felt so proud to have a sister teaching downtown. Sometimes my brothers Dan and Paul dropped me off at the teachers' dormitory for a few hours to visit while they did some shopping or ran errands that took them a couple of hours. I was in a state of pure joy. Loretta came back to her room between classes, since her dorm was right in the schoolyard. The other teachers who were in their rooms always came by to give me books to read and bananas or apples. The doors to Loretta's room and the other teachers' rooms were always open, so I could see right in. There was a living room and kitchen shared by all, and usually two of them shared each bathroom. How they filled those bathrooms up, with strange bottles and jars of every size! What I remember the most is that all of Loretta's friends smiled at me. I felt like I had a half-dozen big sisters all rolled into one.

Our older sister Loretta was a true inspiration. She was smart and pretty and had a wonderful disposition with all of us and with people in general. Loretta was five feet-seven and weighed at least 150 pounds. She was always a little plump, but she had a well-built body with big legs, so she wore very tall high-heeled shoes with her hair swept up on both sides into a cluster of ringlets just off the center of her forehead. Little yellow earrings and rosy red lipstick (when Papa was not around) carried the eye right to her face. Her bright eyes lit with laughter, and she had no reservation about walking up to just about anyone and striking up a conversation. Because Loretta was away at college when I was growing up, I knew the rest of us would go to college, not just because Papa always said we would, but also because Mama's brother, Uncle Sonny, went to Alcorn College and other family members studied elsewhere — aunts and cousins, male and female alike. Loretta was more living evidence that we would carry on the tradition.

Carzella

While Loretta was off at Tougaloo High School, Carzella was the oldest at home, in the ninth grade. Catherine Watts and her sisters lived just a skip and a jump from our house, and they used to love trekking through the thickets of evergreens to find a gum tree so they could chew its sticky, dried sap. Carzella, Catherine and her sisters all liked to smack away, their chewing pace catching up with the tempo

My sister Carzella and her husband, Sam, are shown in 1950 when she was in her first pregnancy. There were eleven more pregnancies after this one.

of their chatter, which was generally about boys and babies. Once in a while, a big truck could be heard way off in the distance, crackling over the gravel road, the driver usually a man we had known from day one or at least remotely. But little did they know that this time the driver had stopped to answer a call from nature.

"Girl, I got a piece of cloth for my blouse from an old curtain Mama took down. It's heavy dark blue — but I'm sewing white lace around the collar to perk it right up," explained Carzella.

"Don't make it too perky," Catherine chimed in. "Don't let it distract too much from that wide waistband around your little tiny waist."

"You mean from that tiny little bare midriff above that tiny little waist," joked Catherine.

"Now hold on, I've gotta be able to wear it to church on Sunday. What if Sam's there?"

"So, Carzella, what of it? You don't think he wants to see those neat little tucks below your bodice nip into your soft, pretty ribs?"

"Oh, come on, he's not that kind of guy. He'll be admiring my new white sandals, or straightening the bow beside my pompadour."

"That's what you think," taunted Catherine. "We've seen him looking at you. Take the Fourth of July. We saw him brush your bangs back when you leaned over to offer him your peanut brittle. What kinda candy do you think he was lookin' at?"

Ellouise and Catherine knew what they were talking about, because they were looking for the same flirtation every Saturday afternoon when they went downtown, strutting up and down the sidewalk in their snug two-piece shirtwaists or princess-cut frocks with swishy skirts and sweetheart necklines, with their hot-combed pageboys and their fingernails painted bright. In and out of the ten-cent stores and the department stores they went, stopping at the Dairy Freeze and the hamburger stand, as if they could think of eating. Downtown was for seeing and being seen, and theirs was the age to do it.

The Accident

In 1942, Clifford set out in Papa's old paper-wood truck with no window in the back and no door on the driver's side to take Carzella into Columbia to buy a plaid wool coat. They were almost there when the traffic got heavier on old Highway 24. Most of the road was straight and smooth, and one stretch had a few curves and small hills, but the two lanes got everybody else downtown. It was Christmas Eve. As they approached the city limits, traffic slowed, and Carzella turned and looked out the open window behind her and saw a Greyhound bus tearing down the highway. Holding onto her seat, her eyes fixed on the truck, she shouted, "Clifford, that bus is coming too fast. It's too fast, Clifford!"

Clifford caught a quick sideways glance and tried to speed up, but it was too late. There was nowhere to pull over on the little two-lane highway, and with the oncoming traffic he had nowhere to go. The bus plowed into the back of Clifford's truck. Broken glass flew everywhere. The impact knocked the truck clear across the road and into an oncoming car filled with white folks. Both the car and the truck came to a dead standstill. Carzella, able to hold on, was jolted and shaken and scared, but Clifford was thrown out and landed with his head between the wheel of the truck and the wheel of the oncoming car. Carzella got out and saw that the white folks were hurt, but not badly. Banged up and bleeding, they saw the Greyhound bus and knew it had hit the truck. They were taken to the hospital at once by spectators. Clifford pulled himself up off the ground and reeled around as if in a crazed, dizzy spell.

The Greyhound bus barreled on down the highway. Next, it struck a colored man's one-horse wagon loaded with corn to sell at the mill. Ears of corn flew into the air and the road and the man on the wagon was killed instantly. The bus kept right on going, coming to a halt only after it hit a fence and tore it down. The news on the radio said the driver, a white man, was drunk. Nothing more was said about him. It was announced that the black man was killed, but had no family that survived him. Uncle Willis came out to our house and talked with Papa about a lawsuit against the Greyhound Company. Papa's answer: the white folks were not hurt badly, and they knew Clifford was not at fault; Carzella and Clifford were not hurt; and everyone would be all right.

By the time she was fifteen, Carzella had fallen in love. She said she knew she would be getting married in a couple of years. She didn't tell anyone in the family about this great love of hers. It came as a total surprise to Mama and Papa two years later, in 1947, when she did tell them.

The one thing Carzella wanted to do most was to fix hair. She wanted that as much as she wanted to get married. So, Papa and Mama sent her out to Hattiesburg when she was in tenth grade to study cosmetology. A cousin, Vera, one of Aunt Sang's daughters, lived there.

Carzella stayed with her, studying at Eureka and Young's Cosmetology on Mobile Street for nine months. She was very good at it during her entire teenage years. It was during the eleventh grade that everything changed. She already knew how to make money. Everybody and anybody got their hair done back then. It was the one thing women had that they could do.

Carzella met her husband, Sammy Lee, in 1945 in the churchyard of St. Paul's Baptist Church on the fourth Sunday of September. She was with Mama and two of her girlfriends, Bobbie and Dorothy. They were walking around the churchyard with Mama. Sam said the first time he saw Mama, he thought she was so pretty to have a big daughter like Carzella. Carzella and Sam liked each other from the start and began courting. They courted mostly through writing, because Sam was drafted into the army for two years. When he returned, they went to Papa and asked him if they could marry. Papa said no at first, explaining that they should wait a few years. Carzella could finish high school — she was only going into the eleventh grade at that time. But they kept on after Papa, to the point that he finally gave in. She'd fallen in love with Sam when she was fifteen, and she had no ears for Papa's insistence that she finish high school before starting a family. So on a balmy night at the end of August 1947, a very romantic event was staged at the Exposé home. The plan was for a small wedding, but in no time headlights and lamp lights filled the moonlight and half the community was gazing upon our front porch waiting for the happy couple.

Rev. Lumzy, the pastor of our church, was all decked out in his black suit and black shoes and black tie against a gleaming white shirt, his manicured fingers wrapped around his prayer book. Loretta and Mondell Lee, Miss Ella's daughter from up the road, were the brides-maids, nervously waiting in the boys' back bedroom while Mama zipped up Carzella's full-length, full-skirted, glow-white chiffon dress and Carzella slipped into her sling-back, open-toed shoes.

"Just wait a minute before you put on your veil," Mama said. It was white netting that Loretta had sewn onto a headband. It fell to

Carzella's shoulders just where the sheer, puffed sleeves of her dress cupped her arms. Cousin Vera, one of Aunt Sang's daughters, had sewn the dress, designing it into a pretty "V" at the neckline to show off Carzella's sweet, doll face framed by a full head of ringlet curls. Sam wore a pin-striped suit and tie the same rich, dark green of late summer foliage and was accompanied by Dennis Otis, his best man and best friend. Sam's sister, Maple, was in attendance with her husband, and Sam's father, though their mother was home sick in bed and sent a big cream cake along with the others. Papa had been ready for hours, sitting on the front porch chewing tobacco, spitting its juice out over the flowers onto the grass.

"Mama, there's a bus full of people out there!" Carzella exclaimed, peeking out the window. "Yes, I know they probably thought it was just the thing to do, being friends of ours. We'll just have to wait until everyone settles somewhere," Mama calmly said. They all came in a big yellow school bus right up into the front yard, which was full of people.

All the way out to the road, a good seventy-five feet from the porch, eight or ten other cars and trucks had arrived from adjoining communities. People sat on the hoods or the roofs of whatever they drove over in, or they leaned against our two big oak trees, or squirmed around the front porch, so that when Carzella entered from the door on one end and Sam from the door on the other end, it was as if they were in spotlights as they proceeded to Rev. Lumzy in the middle and stood at the top of the steps. Carzella held a bouquet Loretta made for her from Mama's old corsages, and it was lovely beneath her radiant smile.

After the big to-do, it was time to eat. Some came to eat as much as to watch the wedding. Banana pudding, pies, cakes, green beans, pan-fried corn, okra, fried chicken and big pots from Miss Ella, and Mary, Aunt Sang, and Aunt Mollie — the regular ones that always were dependable. After the feast, they left and traveled up to Bassfield, Mississippi, where Sam's parents lived, to stay with them. Over the next few years, Papa would load us up on his pickup truck, and he and Mama would head out to Bassfield to visit. Sam's parents lived in a little house way off the main road, on a white man's land, which they farmed.

By June 3, 1950, Carzella started having babies. Larry came first, but as a crawling baby he suffered a severe burn on three-fourths of his head in the ashes of the fireplace. For years, he was taken up to Jackson to the hospital for treatments and many skin grafts. The scars healed up pretty smooth, but he was left with no hair on most of his head. Lynda followed on December 9, 1951, and there would be ten more to come. A lot of boys, seven in all, and five girls. Somehow, Lynda just naturally protected Larry because of the burn on his head. The next four children would be born in the little three-room house Papa built next door to ours, and the last six or so in their new house, built up the road from ours.

Carzella always came down to our house for a few weeks every time she'd have another baby. Myrtis, Jimmy, and I looked forward to taking care of the baby while Carzella slept, especially during the night. She never had to get up to feed the baby or change its diaper. She slept right through. We always had a warm bottle heated up in a pan of water on the stove and a stack of diapers ready in case the baby woke up. I enjoyed it so much. The babies were fat and pretty and didn't cry much. If they did cry, I would stick those bottles in their mouths. Because Carzella's older children were so close to our ages and lived so close to our house, they seemed like they were younger brothers and sisters more than nieces and nephews.

Larry always acted the oldest and would watch after Lynda, but sometimes he'd miss some of the things she was able to get away with. One time, when Lynda was about two, she went into our bathroom and unrolled a whole roll of toilet tissue onto the floor. Darlene went in and did her best to reroll it. But I wasn't so lucky. Another time when Lynda was down at our house she managed to get the top off the Royal Crown hairdressing container and proceeded to dig out all of that hairdressing product and put it into her hair. She had gobs of it in spots and blobs of it hanging on the ends of her hair. It was an awful mess. Then I had to wash her hair to get it all out. Lynda just laughed. She thought it was so funny. It took forever, the rewashing.

As they got older, it was Lynda who watched Larry. She was one year younger and could be fierce. When other little children poked fun at Larry's head, she would bawl them out and be ready to fight in a minute. Those children learned fast not to fool with her. Our sixth grade teacher would not tolerate anyone making fun of Larry, especially since it was a burn that had caused his baldness. In the late 1960s, Larry and Lynda went to the newly integrated all-white Improve High School. The students were no different when it came to poking fun. After the third or fourth day, a white student made fun of Larry's head. Lynda was right there and told that white boy off in no uncertain terms that he better leave her brother alone.

"Do you hear me?" she said. That boy took one look at Lynda and her mean face and never said another word. Larry was nudging Lynda all the time to come on, leave it alone. Lynda finally did agree with Larry, but told him she had to do it. She loved her brother and protected him. Larry would not get into any verbal confrontation. He held his head high and walked tall like he was raised to do, even when the white students refused to sit next to him in class. He sat all alone on one side of the classroom, until finally, one white boy, and later, a white girl, sat next to him. Somehow there is always someone in the group who does what is right and fair.

Going up to Carzella's was somewhere for me to go anytime when we were not working, even at nighttime. I'd make me a fire torch with a big piece of lighter wood. Sometimes I'd cover the end of it with an old rag wrapped around it. It put out good light. Because it was not too far — four or five hundred feet straight through the woods — I'd get there in no time, walking or running a little. But it was not because I was scared. A clear path went straight through. I'd just sit around there for a while and come back down to our house.

The Mischief Group

I never saw so many things children could get into down at our house. They repeated things that we had done when we were three and four years old — like going through Papa's overall pockets and always finding a nickel or dime. It was like the lost and found. Sometimes, I wondered if Papa didn't leave change in there deliberately because he knew we went through his pockets, as did his grandchildren years later.

With every generation of children, there are always some in the family who are just like the ones before them — one or two just like Grandpa Daniel, or Uncle so-and-so, making fun, imitating the preachers, telling lies and being scary. Grandpa Daniel's great-grandson, Gregory, was so much like him when it came to causing pure fear in his brothers and sisters.

The same path I used to take going up to Carzella's house is the one my nieces and nephews took coming down to our house, also at any time — noontime, late afternoon, or dusk dark. As four- to seven-year-olds Larry, Lynda, Gregory, and Mike would set off walking down to our house, right through the woods without a care in the world. The sounds that could be heard were unreal — different kinds of birds, early evening crickets, frogs, rabbits, snakes — good hunting for the cats.

Greg always managed to stir up more noise. As soon as they got into the thickest brush and the path got a little bit narrow, he would rattle the limbs, make some god-awful animal sound, and swear it was a bear. I see him coming out of the bushes. He's running behind me: "Run, run, get out of the way, we gonna get caught," out of breath, screaming and hollering all the way to our house. Jimmy and I could hear the noise and knew who it was. We went out to the edge of the yard right by the road and waited for them. Mama and Papa got an earful of them being chased by a bear. All Jimmy and I could do was laugh, because Grandpa Daniel scared us up at his house with that same bear in the woods. That bear stayed hidden until Grandpa Daniel's

94

great grandchildren stirred him up again. Once they got down to the house, they would all go out to the barn and poke at the hogs and pigs through the pen with a stick, or at the chickens through the chicken wire. They had to always be doing something around the house, inside or out.

My older brothers smoked, as did other grown folks, but Papa didn't — he just chewed tobacco. They saw all these grown folks smoking, and somehow knew they could do the same thing. Our front porch was high up off the ground, and it was easy for us as young children to go under the house and play in the dirt. Darlene and I used to go under there when Jimmy practiced on the piano since we had to get out of the house.

One particular afternoon, Lynda, Greg, and Mike decided to amuse themselves. They went to Clifford's room to see what smoking a cigarette was all about. They took a box of matches and a Camel cigarette and crawled under the house. Lighting the cigarette, they passed it around, taking puffs. Mama was busy in the kitchen and not concerned about them. They would never want Mama and Papa — or their parents, and Carzella, and Sam — to know what they were doing. Trying to keep quiet was hard, and when Lynda started coughing and choking, things got worse. They figured they had to get out from under the house or they would be in deep trouble. Not uttering a single word, they calmly walked back home up the road. The thought that they might set something on fire under the house never entered their minds. Mama did notice that they had left, but she kept right on in the kitchen. Just like the time when Darlene and I got into Mama's chocolates that turned out to be Ex-lax, she knew exactly who did what.

One day when Lynda was down to our house she was feeling pretty adventurous— adventurous enough to take a dip of Mama's Barrett's snuff she always kept on the fireplace mantle. I don't know what was on Lynda's mind, except all her young life she'd seen Mama dip snuff and must have wondered what it tasted like. Mama was totally unaware of what Lynda was doing, and Lynda definitely didn't plan on telling her. It made her so sick sweat was popping out on her forehead and her head was swimming so fast she thought she would pass out and die. When Mama asked what was wrong, she had to come clean. Mama gave her some cold water to wash out her mouth. Lynda never allowed her curiosity to get the best of her again.

Our grandparents were an extension of our own parents. Going to their house was like home, but the big difference was that we could do almost anything. They never whipped us. They always had something different and good to eat, like strawberries. Their front porch was bigger — it ran across the front and down one side — a bigger place to run and play, to feel safe and loved. Comfort and freedom wrapped into one.

Chapter 4

Horse and Buggy Courtship

"I Could 'a Been Your Daddy"

The sad and sober congregation was gathered to share the loss of their beloved. Etta Mae Dukes was laid out at her funeral, as peaceful as she had been all her living years. There was hardly a dry eye to be found in the church. Even the hymns were sung halfway as shoulders shuddered and throats sobbed. A tall figure stood all alone at the back of the church, carrying seventy-eight years of force along with him. In his tan suit and vest topping a pin-striped shirt and his Sunday-best brown shoes, he strutted down the aisle, flaunting a baritone voice as commanding as his manly physique. "This is no time to be mournful," he proclaimed. "We are here to celebrate our beloved."

Some held their hats on their heads and turned. Everyone in sight gawked at the stranger. A few recognized him as the Reverend Stallsworth, an old-time preacher from Lampton, near Columbia, where he had been actively involved in organizing the sit-ins of the civil rights movement. Woolworth's, lunch counters, and soda fountains—he'd been there, in the worst and the best of ways. Stallsworth picked up the funeral announcement and read from its page:

> And God shall wipe away all tears from their eyes and there shall be no more death, neither sorrow nor crying. Neither shall there be any more pain [Revelations 21:24].

Etta Mae Dukes died on a quiet, cold, but clear day in February 1976. The verse unleashed by the Reverend's voice rang through the church with unforgettable clarity. "Her passing pointed to more than one of the free souls she had honored with her beauty. Let us now go back to the days when many a suitor, known or undeclared, took his notice of her bud in bloom."

From the beginning, Papa was farming with his parents on their own land, and so were many Negro families. Young people were flirting, chasing each other, and marrying, each couple raising a house full of children. After most of the crops were gathered on Papa's farm, he went with his brother, Luther, to Arkansas to work in the sawmills, along with a few men from the neighborhood and nearby Columbia and Hattiesburg. They had heard about jobs in towns and cities outside of Mississippi.

Around the same time, Papa had heard about those "pretty Dukes girls" down at the Columbia Valley Methodist Church, a wood-slat building of natural cedar crowned with two handsome steeples with shingled roofs. Located just off Owens Street, a wide avenue running down the predominantly Negro section of Columbia, the church was founded in 1908 with only six members by Emanuel Dukes, Mama's father, who became its minister.

Also an avid fisherman and carpenter, Dukes was a farmer who had married Sophronia Jefferson from the Hub community in 1879, and they had brought nine children into the world, six of them being the brightest blossoms in any spring bouquet. Not only that, Emanuel allowed them to shoot rifles and hunt squirrels, rabbits, and fowl with their brothers. While both parents were strong disciplinarians, they were not overly stern; and other delightful privileges were granted their daughters, such as driving the A-model Ford. Gentlemen callers stood in line to beg the hand of each of the Dukes girls as they blushed in return.

One Sunday, Papa decided to take his horse and buggy over to visit the church. On that summer day of 1912, Mama was at the service with her father, Rev. Emanuel Dukes, the pastor, and also her mother, Sophronia, and her sisters Roxanna and Gladys. During the few minutes between Sunday school and the regular service, they were out in the churchyard, standing in the shade of the old oak tree, laughing and talking, when Mama noticed a young man stuck on her smile. He was beside himself, grinning quietly from ear to ear, but he finally pulled his pitter-patter heart together and sauntered over to the ladies. As he approached, Mama dropped her jaws and gasped, and when he came over she wondered what to say to him.

Noah was glowing with hope that the pretty young girl would talk to him. "Good morning, how are you?" he managed to get out, but in his nervousness he continued talking without waiting for a reply, introducing himself as Noah Henry Exposé. Mama answered by saying her name, all prim and proper, and those of her sisters Roxanna and Gladys. Papa extended his hand, but in a heartbeat, it was time to go back inside the church for the next service. Mama and her sisters sat in the front row because their father, being the minister, had to be able to cast his gaze on his own children, for inspiration as well as for disciplinary purposes, no matter how many of them were at church that Sunday. During this era, there was only one church service per month, and it was on every second Sunday.

A few weeks passed before Papa and Mama saw each other again, and in all that time the only thing Noah Henry Exposé thought about was the pretty Dukes girl. In the meantime, Mama worked in her father's field along with her two sisters and brother. They all still lived at home and took turns doing the chores around the house. Her three older sisters and three older brothers were either away at school or married, having left home to start their own families.

Papa, on the other hand, had only one brother, Luther, and between them they had a very fancy buggy their father had helped them buy. Drawn by one horse, it had no hood, and it could seat four people with its slightly elevated backseat. The exterior was black and it showed off the glowing seats of red leather. The body was almost square, or box-like, about five feet long and four feet wide, with a cut-out area for the wheels to make sharp turns to the right or left. Now the buggy was light as a feather, so the horse that drew it could fly like an eagle down the lonely, country road and whip up a whirlwind.

Papa kept the pretty chestnut horse brushed down and well fed. He and Luther would get all dressed up on a Sunday to go courting. Not only did they step out into their own neighborhood — First Hopewell Baptist Church, Little River, or Improve, Blue Spring, Rose Hill — but they also ventured out to Friendship Baptist Church, Foxworth, and John the Baptist Church. Ten miles or more from their own home, all of these communities had churches where people from any of these neighborhoods gathered on a Sunday. Papa felt that because his father owned land and he worked on his father's farm and had his own horse and buggy, he might stand a chance of winning the pretty Dukes girl's favor.

Truth to tell, Mama had another suitor at this time, and he also had a horse and buggy. This buggy was a two-seater with no raised area in the back. It had no hood either, and it was emerald green wood with a golden interior. The handsome horse that drew it was known as "Sugar," and his name was chanted and cheered on top of hoots and hollers and hoofbeats that kicked up the dust at a picnic on the church grounds one fine day. The race was on, the green and gold two-seater against the black and red four-seater, and each one hightailed it over the old country road, raising white hankies as they rounded the bend. Sugar pranced over the finish line with the emerald cart in tow, but not before Noah's horse and buggy crossed the goal — and most concurred that the race was not all Noah Exposé won on that fine day.

The Bells Are Ringing

A month later, on the next second–Sunday at church, Papa sat three rows in back of Mama. She hadn't seen him enter, and at one point she turned around to peer through the crowd for his face. He caught

100

her by surprise and, embarrassed, she turned back around in a flash, because, for one thing, she knew that if her father saw her facing the back of the church, she would be in for a good scolding for irreverence and vanity.

Emanuel was a man of fine fabric — of character, integrity, and proper decorum — an imposing figure, standing proud with his stocky body, sharp nose, and thin lips. Because he was a minister of the church, he felt his children had to behave better than other children in the congregation. He had devoted his life to the church; on principle, he wanted his family to behave as a walking testament of his faith. Sophronia and the children were expected to set an example for others.

When Papa was courting Mama he won a horse and buggy race with another of Mama's suitors. Papa won both the race and Mama's hand in marriage. They are shown here in their wedding photograph in 1917.

As soon as the service ended, Papa made his way over to Mama. With reserve and gentility, he put out his plea — to talk with her Pa about coming over to visit. She could only blush, and Grandpa said he could. But most amazing of all was the snow-white hair that capped the handsome face of the minister. He was a walking legend in the community because his hair

101

had turned white before he turned thirty years old. It was the same with his father, brothers, and sisters, and the gene would continue on down throughout the Dukes family.

One way of putting it is to say that from a child's point of view, he was a spook. This could be observed in the rambunctious talk of the neighborhood children as they picked cucumbers, climbed up and down the sugarcane mill, and played hide and seek in the barn. From time to time, the Lee boys and girls would mimic Emanuel Dukes as Casper the Friendly Ghost. In the late evenings as it grew dark and their parents sat out on their porch dipping snuff, they stretched their twilight games in and out of the smokehouse, mimicking Emanuel Dukes as their target in blind man's bluff. Did it have something to do with his yellow skin? His hair was silky and soft. When his sisters came up from New Orleans to visit, everyone thought they were white. But we are running away from our story, because we have left tenderhearted Papa poised to embrace his young sweetheart, at least with his longing eyes leaping from their sockets.

The next time Papa stood on the church grounds, Mama arrived with her family in their horse and buggy. Her father was joined by her mother and her two sisters Roxanna and Gladys. Papa was less intimidated by the great-looking man, but deferred to him out of respect. He rushed over to greet them, making sure he first said good morning to her parents. They said good morning back, almost in unison. Emanuel told Papa he could come see Mama after church.

They all went inside, took their seats, and were very quiet. No one looked toward the back of the church, and certainly no one giggled. Papa sat a few rows behind Mama and her sisters, enjoying the devotional, the hymns, the choir singing, and the preaching and forgetting about Mama for the moment—or at least he tried to. Overall, this Methodist service was not too different from Papa's Baptist church service. It was a little less active and more conservative, without the shouting and clapping and "amens" Papa was used to.

Composed and forthright, the serious young caller followed the

Dukes family home in his horse and buggy. After parking his rig under a tree, he walked onto the front porch and sat on the swing next to Emanuel and Sophronia in their rocking chairs. Baby girl Gladys made some lemonade and they all drank the cool summer juice. The father asked the suitor only a few questions: about his parents, their farm, and where it was located. There would be no serious business going on for a while, because Mama was only fifteen years old. She would need to be twenty before she could even think about wedding bells. Finally, Emanuel and Sophronia got up and went inside the house. All the father had to do was look at his daughter, and she knew what it meant. Saying his good-byes, Papa knew he would have to leave soon.

The minute the parents went inside, leaving the three girls out on the porch with Papa, Mama's youngest brother, Artis, came by in his horse and buggy. He jumped out, dressed in a gleaming white suit (he always wore white). Artis wanted to know whose fancy horse and buggy was parked in front of the house.

"That belongs to me," said Papa, standing up.

"Well that sure is a fancy one, if I ever saw one," replied Artis, who was called Shug. He plopped himself on the front porch, poured himself a tall glass of lemonade, and pretended not to notice that the man was there courting. Yet, Shug's presence actually added some ease to the situation, because he was feeling good and looking good, and he was crazy about his sisters.

"Well Noah, let me tell you something," Shug grinned. You got the right church, an' you're in the right pew. Now all you gotta do is move around in it!" The playboy let out a hardy laugh that would have embarrassed the suitor if he hadn't had his own mouth wide open for all the ice breaking he could get.

The two sweethearts courted for the next five years. This gave Papa a chance to get to know Mama's brothers and sisters— one in particular, the oldest, Sarah, whom everyone called Sang, and her husband, Hark, a carpenter and brick mason. Papa, who was always eager to learn everything he could to earn a living, was impressed with Hark's skills. So it was from Uncle Hark that he learned bricklaying and carpentry.

One Sunday after church, Papa went by Mama's house, tied his horse to a tree, straightened out his suit jacket, and knocked on the front door.

"Reverend Dukes, I was wondering if I could take Etta Mae out for a Sunday afternoon drive in my horse and buggy — and of course, one of her sisters would come along, too."

"Well, if Gladys goes along, and you have them back here before dark."

"Etta Mae, you and Gladys come here," he called. Papa had stepped back a little and Grandpa was now standing on the front porch. The whole family stepped onto the porch. "If you girls would like to go out for a ride, get your wraps," instructed Emanuel.

Gladys hopped into the back and stretched out her arms across the top of the seat and rested her head there. As soon as they had gone far enough that they were out of sight, she lit up a cigarette and puffed away.

"I guess Pa's never seen you smoking," admonished Mama. "Ma would just take the pack away from you." Papa got out his chewing tobacco and offered a piece to Mama.

"No, thanks. Shug and Tobey chew sometimes. Gladys takes after our brothers with that smoking."

She was a little nervous, which made her very talkative — church talk, school talk, family talk. All were perfectly acceptable topics. Aunt Gladys just sat back, crossed her legs, and enjoyed one cigarette after another, blowing smoke out into the clear spring day. They'd gone only about a mile or two from home when Papa turned his buggy right around and headed back so as not to squander too much of a good thing. He also wanted to make a good impression on his girl's father.

Papa and Mama saw each other once every month or two, usually at church and occasionally at Mama's house afterwards. After half a year, Grandpa and Grandma decided to pay a visit out to Little River, to Papa's First Hopewell Baptist Church, which held its regular service every third Sunday because the pastor served more than one church as pastor. During the service, Sophronia Dukes sat next to Eran Exposé just beneath the pulpit, in front of the other sisters of the church. The Reverend Emanuel Dukes led a prayer just before the sermon began.

After the service, the Dukes family followed the Exposés back up to their house. They all sat on the front porch with tea cakes and milk. The adults talked about church and farming, carpentry and bricklaying, and all that Hark or anyone could teach Papa. Emanuel realized that his daughter would eventually be marrying this young man, but she would have to wait a bit.

During this time an interesting parallel event was occurring behind the scenes. Papa had an affair with a woman from nearby Hattiesburg, and a child was born and named Leola. By 1917, when Papa and Mama got married, this daughter was six years old. Since he wanted to be entirely open with his fiancée, Papa told her about this woman and their child and everything else he'd gotten into before he knew her. Wisely, she reasoned that if it had happened before she knew him it was his business and his responsibility to answer for it honorably.

The day finally came when the Reverend Dukes blessed the proposal of Noah Exposé to marry Etta Mae Dukes. It was December 31, 1917, and our country was entering the last year of what would be known as World War I. It was also the last day of the year, a year of hope and dreams and restlessness for Etta Mae. In the Dukes tradition, she was a woman with a head on her shoulders. And, in general, she was a woman of great resolve, never finding herself of two minds about anything. But before her was the rest of her life. Was she on the right course for putting together her many talents? She walked through the church doorway, drawing all eyes to her magnificent presence.

The wedding was performed by Grandpa Emanuel in his church, Columbia Valley United Methodist. First, he walked his daughter down the aisle. Then he took his place in front of the bride and groom and performed the simple ceremony. The family filled half the church and the farmers of the community filled the rest. The women gasped when they saw the beautiful white gown Mama wore and how well her brothers and sisters were dressed.

Back at the Dukes home, a crowd gathered. People were outside walking around under the trees and down the gravel paths—all waiting for the wedding party to return. Children ran about and played. Inside, someone played the piano nonstop. All of Mama's brothers and sisters, Papa's family, uncles and aunts, grandma and grandpa, were there. Uncle Shug had his fishing and hunting buddies over, and his ever present flask of whiskey was inside his coat pocket.

The food festival was on Grandma Sopronia's sister, Aunt Polly. She was a natural for cooking and cook-outs. Fried rabbit, fish, frog legs, collards, black-eyed peas, cornbread, turnips, peach cobbler, pecan pies, pound cakes. Neighbors and other relatives added to the bounty of food.

You're in the Army Now

The new couple lived with the groom's parents for about six months until Papa was drafted into the army on June 18, 1918. He was stationed at Camp Grant in Rockford, Illinois, and remained in the army for one year. The barrack housed hundreds of men with recreation rooms, and a kitchen. Papa worked as a cook and baked more loaves of fresh bread each day in the huge army ovens than he'd ever imagined. He was told that the officers ate the same food as the privates in their mess hall. During that time, Mama alternated between staying with her parents and with Papa's parents. She was still responsible for her share of the cooking, washing, cleaning, and fieldwork, and she did whatever was expected of her that she was physically capable of doing through her pregnancy and childbirth. The oldest of the first four of my brothers, Noah Jr., was born on September 25, 1918, with Tootsie, Clifford, and Bufford to follow.

Mama worked alongside Papa in the fields every day when he returned from the army. She was strong, and hard work was not new to her. She did everything except plow with a mule. When my older brothers were still little, she would spread out one of her quilts on the grass under a tree at the field's edge, or she would put the baby in a wagon Papa had built, all padded with a quilt, with bottles of milk and pieces of fruit for the bigger boys. They played, slept, and cried, and Mama stopped from time to time to check on them. When it was time to cook, she just gathered them up, and back to the house they went.

Every year, Papa planted a few more acres of cotton, and every year he bought a few more acres of land. Mama could pick 400 pounds of cotton a day. Meanwhile, she did all her own cleaning and raised the children along with Papa. They both disciplined my brothers. As the boys got older,

Papa in the Army. World War I, 1918.

they worked alongside Papa and Mama, doing whatever they could based on their ages and sizes. They picked up potatoes, pulled corn, gathered peanuts and cut sugarcane, milked cows, slopped hogs, and watered the mules, cows, and hogs in the barn. As young boys, Noah Jr., Tootsie, and Clifford would go out to Hattiesburg sometimes and work in the paper mill, as would a lot of other young men from our neighborhood.

Leola, Papa's daughter, was by then a young girl. My brother Tootsie

107

said Papa would bring her out to our house to visit and they would play with her — shooting marbles, mostly. Leola liked being out on the farm, going to the barn, looking at the cows, mules, chickens, and hogs; she hated leaving to go back to the big city of Hattiesburg. Leola got married when she was young to a man whose last name was Moffett. Tootsie said he and Clifford would visit Leola in Hattiesburg until after she got married. But when the war ended, Moffet and Leola moved to Detroit, where he got a better job in a car plant.

It was 1961 and winter in Michigan, and snow was everywhere. I'd never seen snow like that. When I was a child, it had snowed only one time. The flakes were so light that when they hit the ground, they were practically melted. But this snow was a different story. Just getting out of the car was an ordeal, and the shoes I had on weren't the most suitable. An old family friend had brought me up to Muskegon, Michigan. To my surprise, I met Leola, her son Bubba, and her daughter Nettie Merle. The resemblance was strong between us. Leola looked just like Papa and so did her two children. Bubba had Papa's head, like so many of the boys in the family: grand-boys and even great-grand-boys. Leola and Nettie Merle looked like two or three of us girls. It was quite an interesting resemblance.

That afternoon, Bubba took me around to a couple of his friends' houses, and to a little eatery where he hung out — all the time saying this is my aunt, holding my hand and grinning from ear to ear. He just showed me off. I was younger than him and some of his buddies didn't believe him. Bubba enjoyed it. It was fun for me, and I was so glad to come face to face with a half-sister. At twenty-two, being that far from home was quite an experience. As the years went by, I would hear about them and finally news of them stopped. I never saw them again.

Chapter 5

Church-Going

Going to church was the biggest regular social event for us country folks. Every third Sunday, a week before the end of the month, it was as constant as working in the fields every day until Saturday noon. The prayer meetings on Wednesday night, Sunday school before the church service, and choir practice anytime during the week kept us all on the right track.

Sunday was a relief and a rest for our bodies and minds. We'd all be saved and healed on the third Sunday until the next time. Meeting up with classmates and friends was just as important as the church service and something to look forward to— almost as much as the adult choir's music. The hymns were as good, and sometimes better, if led by a deacon who could sing well. Some prayers were good, and some not so good— some people couldn't pray too good, just like leading hymns. It was nothing for us to make fun of everything when we got back to the house. Myrtis and I would laugh in a minute; Jimmy would be more serious. Of course, Mama would hear us and tell us to "shush up." The sermon was always good. The Reverend Lumzy was a great preacher.

The other entertainment highlights of that day were the women all dressed up in their Sunday go-to-church clothes. Every type of dress, suit, or frock you can imagine, every style, color and size. Hats going in all directions, some looking like they were on backward. Gloves and pocketbooks, high-heeled shoes hurting many feet— and not all matching, either. I'd sit on the edge of my seat looking around to watch all the activity. When we saw something funny, we'd roll our eyes and snicker, putting our heads down and covering our mouths, because if Mama saw us we'd be in deep trouble.

This particular Sunday, the sermon was "David and Bathsheba." It could not have been a better fit, because I knew there were rumors of men in the neighborhood who were after other men's wives. It was about King David, who saw a woman taking a bath. He wanted her and saw to it that her husband was sent off to war, surely to be killed. He was, and being the king, David knew he could have the wife for himself, and he did. The Rev. Lumzy spoke of religion and Christianity having to be real. To forsake what was not yours—how you can't have everything you want, even though you've seen a good-looking woman.

The humming, praying and soft amens echoed throughout the church. There were weeping eyes all around, heads nodding up and down, and patting feet. It seemed this sermon stirred up a lot in more than just the women who were up and shouting, but the ones sitting down too. I wondered if some were already after some man, not their husbands, and felt guilty about getting caught. Some people shouted and wanted forgiveness when they did wrong. To me, it meant that they were not supposed to be running after other men's wives, no matter how pretty they were. Or that the ones we saw at the ballgames or at church functions or downtown on Saturday afternoons better not flirt with us young girls—because if they did, I could not wait to tell Papa about it. That gave me a chance to make a fuss to him about having to go to church so much. Everything was about the church. The sermon also meant not letting my girlfriends talk me into letting a boy feel my breasts behind the school bus at the ballgames, and definitely not letting them kiss me.

The sermon was building up, and by the time the Rev. Lumzy got to the height of his sermon, there were three or four women up on their feet shouting from different corners in the church. The same two or three women every time. It was downright fun to watch the deacons watch the women shouting. It never failed. The same deacons would get up and console the shouting women. Big bosoms flopping up and down, the deacons holding the women to keep from hurting themselves. The ever-present "women in white," the usher board, all lined up in the back of the church. They kept their uniforms starched white with pretty colorful handkerchiefs in the upper left pocket. Fans waved everywhere, colorful ones even from funeral homes. The women in white would also console the shouting women. Getting everybody seated before and during the service was the easy part. The shouting women kept all of us on the edge of our seats. Arms flaring, knees buckling, some looked like they were hitting the deacons in the chest, and it was very entertaining.

The tempo slowed down. Less noise and the shouting turned to whimpers. The Rev. Lumzy would open the doors of the church for anyone to join the church, singing "Come to Jesus. His voice was big and full of rhythm. Weeping eyes all around and the amens dying down. Sometimes, one or two people would join the church, and sometimes not.

The collection followed, with two deacons called upon, and all of us marching around, putting what money we had on the table. Everyone saw what others put on the table. The ushers would pass a plate around to the ones who remained seated. The choir sang an upbeat song because we were all uplifted from the shouting and the sermon. It was stimulating and joyful, the whole service, and it made me feel good. My favorite hymn of all was "I Heard the Voice of Jesus Say." It was worth going to church for that alone. That hymn was led by one of the deacons before the sermon:

> *I heard the voice of Jesus say, "Come unto Me and rest,*
> *Lay down, thou weary one,*
> *Lay down Thy head upon My breast!"*
> *I came to Jesus as I was, weary, and worn, and sad;*
> *I found in Him a resting place, and He has made me glad.*

111

The Reverend Willie Lewis "Uncle Claude" Lumzy had been pastor of First Hopewell as long as I could remember. Being big and robust, he talked in a kind and gentle voice, never mean. I was never scared of him because he was the preacher. A family man and local farmer, he did what all the other farmers did, farm the land. He was very active in the community and involved in education. He operated the first Head Start program in Marion County out of Christian Union Church, an attempt to prepare colored children of preschool age for regular school. In later years, he operated a little grocery store, just about where our softball field and shop was in high school, the site of La Marion High. The other thing about the Rev. Lumzy was that he was about the only other adult that could discipline us.

As juniors in the church, we had our own association. We selected our own preacher as our president, but he had to be approved by the deacons. The Reverend Ollie Spates was our preacher. We'd put on programs and he preached. We all had specific duties and the service ran just like the adult service. Our junior choir sang, and the money we collected went into a fund kept by the adult Home Mission Society. It paid for our travels to other churches to sing as the guest choir.

Jimmy was our pianist and listening to her was like listening to someone on TV or the radio playing, but she was my sister. She not only played religious songs, but also boogie-woogie, as well as "Moonlight Sonata" and "Für Elise" by Beethoven, and "Flight of the Bumblebee." When we were little, Darlene and I had to go outside and play when Jimmy practiced because Mama wanted total quiet in the house. Mama and Papa would sit out on the front porch in their rockers and just listen, patting their feet. We could not touch Jimmy's music books either. When I got older, I would drive her down to Lampton High School, about ten miles east of us and one of our more frequent competitors in basketball. The music teacher there was Miss Bess. Where she came from, I don't know, but she was the very best music teacher around all these parts.

Papa knew Professor Pittman, the athletic director there, and I found out about her through him. Jimmy was already playing piano and reading some music by seventh grade. So for the next five years, she studied under Miss Bess. Our Saturday morning field "things" (scrap cotton, stump clearing, and trash) were sometimes missed by Jimmy because she was at music practice. Miss Bess could also sing and Jimmy had a real good alto voice.

The radio station in Columbia had local junior and senior choirs come to sing on some Sunday mornings. The manager of the station had heard about us and even sent someone out to listen to us sing in our church. The result was that our Junior Choir of First Hopewell Baptist Church was invited to sing once a month for three months. By traveling to sing in other communities, we made a name for ourselves, mostly because our lead singer was so naturally talented and everyone knew that she could sing better than any young girl her age, or most older women, far and near. Our neighbor was the best male singer around for all our times.

My sister Jimmy, our pianist, would get us all together on the Friday night before the Sunday we were to perform so that we could practice and choose what songs we would sing on the radio. The announcer told Jimmy that the program would be fifteen minutes long and we could sing three songs.

Not everybody showed up for practice on Friday nights, but a few faithful ones always did — Jimmy, of course, our lead singer, three other girls, and me. Jimmy sang background and so did the other four of us, making two altos and two sopranos. Without fail, we six were always there to put together the radio program numbers. It was never a problem with the songs because we had a strong leader and strong back-up singers.

During those years of singing in the choir, I learned that it takes as few as three to make a good sound, unless it's a duet or a solo, but six was always a good number for a group. Usually, I drove Papa's car to pick up the other girls, then we were on our way down to the radio station. The station was actually less than a mile outside of downtown

Columbia, and it was set back away from other buildings and off the road.

Once we had arrived and parked in the small lot, we went into the station. We had at least fifteen minutes before it was time to go on, and we sat there, outside the booth, where we could see the announcer going on with the program that was already in progress. As the time came closer for us to perform, he would motion for us to come in. Jimmy was at the piano and the rest of us gathered around the microphone. We had to be perfectly quiet because it was a live broadcast and all the microphones were on in the broadcast room.

I had led songs in church before this, so I was not nervous— well, maybe just a little — but once we got started I wasn't nervous at all. The minute Jimmy hit the first note, all the nervous feelings were gone. The announcer would say, "And now, I bring to you, the First Hopewell Baptist Church Junior Choir. They will sing for you 'Move on Up a Little Higher,' which has been sung by one of the world's greatest gospel singers, Mahalia Jackson."

Jimmy started to play, and all I could think of was to sing as well as I could to be a strong voice to support the leader. On the first number, Jimmy sang alto and so did I, with one girl singing alto and the other two singing soprano. It was a good balance. To sing for a radio audience made us sing better than we did in church or school. There, we could sing until we got it right, but there was no room to make up for mistakes on the air.

The song I often led in church and on that Sunday on the air was "Sweet By and By." After the announcer advertised a couple of products, such as Dial soap and Stop deodorant, he introduced the song as the second tune:

> *There's a land that is fairer than day,*
> *and by faith we can see it afar,*
> *For the Father waits over the way*
> *to prepare us a dwelling place there.*
> *In the sweet by and by,*

we shall meet on that beautiful shore:
In the sweet by and by,
we shall meet on that beautiful shore.
We shall sing on that beautiful shore,
the melodious songs of the blest,
And our spirits shall sorrow no more.
Not a sigh for the blessing of rest.
In the sweet by and by,
we shall meet on that beautiful shore.
In the sweet by and by,
we shall meet on that beautiful shore.

I had practiced enough, it seemed, but when it comes time to perform, you always wonder if it is enough. I started on my cue and the motion from Jimmy, and the song went well, I thought. The last number we did was a group song, "Touch Me, Lord Jesus," with leader; and with that song, we closed out our fifteen-minute broadcast.

The announcer took a few minutes to thank the First Hopewell Baptist Church Junior Choir and to tell us he looked forward to hearing us again. We didn't have to listen to the radio or watch TV to know how good our singers were. Their voices told the story and everybody listened. Their voices were clear and strong without any straining or microphones. The sound came from the bottom of their stomachs. There was some envy and jealousy from the adult choir, but we didn't mind, and we didn't care at all.

The Revival

Our regular church service every third Sunday was like a preview that led up to the yearly one-week revival. All the dressing up for church was nothing compared to the revival. The third Sunday in September was the beginning of the revival. The Rev. Lumzy would preach the Sunday morning service and a visiting minister would preach the Sunday evening service. After the morning service, the biggest serving

115

of food to the whole congregation took place — a couple of hundred at least. According to some folks, a lot of people came just to eat.

Outside, in back of the church, Papa had built a little wooden shed years earlier. It had two tables, the same length as the shed on a concrete slab, ten by twenty-and-a-half feet. The sisters could stand side by side one line behind the table and serve the food to all those hungry church-going folks. The sisters paired up (Mama and Aunt Mollie) usually, and the brightly colored aprons, big spoons, and knives to cut all those cakes came out. Chicken and dumplings was Mama's favorite, as it was for a lot of folks. Other big pots and pans held collard greens, black-eyed peas, sweet corn, okra, potato salad, green beans, banana pudding, fried chicken, cakes of all kind, all sorts of pies, and a lot of pop. The sisters of the church had a big job feeding all those people, and every year it happened again.

The Rev. Lumzy would choose a preacher to run the revival for the week, Monday through Friday. We all waited and wondered who it would be and if he would be a really good preacher. Various community churches were invited to lead the prayer meeting before the sermon and to take up the collection on a specific night. Some of the more local ones came back on other nights—friends of our community folks and others, all farmers alike.

The other big decision made by the sisters of the church was where the visiting preacher would stay for the week. To our surprise and wonderment, Mama agreed to have him stay with us—an unforgettable experience. A big black man from Jackson, Mississippi, was brought down to our house by the Rev. Lumzy at noontime on a Monday. The Reverend Williams was tall, with a mouthful of the whitest teeth. He was friendly and talked to us children, mostly about school. His voice was warm and he had a nice smile. He would be considered good-looking, I think. Anyway, before he came, we had to clean that bedroom from top to bottom, and Mama told us all the things we could not do while he was here.

First, there was no playing the boogie-woogie on the piano. We could not make any noise in the house during the day or night. The radio had to be turned down low and we certainly could not stay up late at night and watch TV, because our TV was in the living room right next to that bedroom. It felt like we couldn't do much of anything. The only thing that made us, especially me and Jimmy, wish he wasn't there was that he talked to us all the time. He had gone to college and I guess he thought he had to use some of that education on us. We liked him after a day or so.

To take some of the cooking responsibility off Mama, one of the sisters in the community would cook early dinner for the preacher every day. One of us (or Papa sometimes) would drive Mama and the preacher over to a different woman's house to eat. We'd be in school most of the day but out early enough to go to dinner. The Rev. Williams got the farmer's wife's cooking more than he imagined, I think. Collard greens, fried corn, fried chicken, sweet potato pie, smothered pork chops, okra, and much more. One time, when Mama and Darlene were over at one of the sister's house to eat with the preacher, Darlene must have been hungry that day, because she got a chicken bone stuck in her throat. The sister got up and came around to Darlene's chair, put her finger down her throat, and pulled it out without a problem.

The one time Papa asked the Rev. William how he enjoyed sister so-and-so's dinner, he said that some food speaks for itself. We thought that was funny and knew exactly who he was talking about. There were a few not-so-good cooks. The services were uplifting, and the way he spoke and explained things in the Bible made him sound like a school-teacher sometimes, or a principal, before he got into the hard-core fire and brimstone of preaching. Everybody talked about it during the week and liked it.

Every few years or so, there would be a big Baptist convention, usually in another state, and a couple of the deacons and the preachers would go. I remember Papa going to it one time in Texas. He was gone only a few days. What I remember the most was us sitting out on the front porch with Mama on the afternoon he came home, and he kissed

Mama. You would have thought he had gone out of the country because it seemed like a long time.

Mama and Papa were always at home together. Mama and Papa were not touchy, kissy types, but they would talk quietly and always say, "Your Papa love you all, and you're good children." They didn't hesitate to defend us in anything. Sometimes in early evening, Mama would lie down across the bed and Papa would brush her white hair. We'd be on the floor, Jimmy and I looking in the Alden's or Sears Roebuck catalogue. Mama was a gentle mama — no screaming and hollering went on in the house. She didn't get all flustered. Usually calm. It took a lot to make her angry, but she knew how to stand up to anybody, and would. She stood her ground when she had to.

Papa was one of the oldest deacons in the church and he had something to say and was involved with every decision that was made in church. The important stuff: to get a preacher for our church, or to get rid of the preacher, if needed, or how the church was run, to select officers. Any carpentry work on the church, he'd do for free. That's what he was, dependable, responsible, and always fair. Papa would sit down and talk to work things out. With us, he would listen to anything if we told him about any deacon or other men in the church we saw at ballgames or in downtown Columbia at the honky-tonks, or at other churches we visited.

Papa and Uncle Luther grew up in the church, and with a mama who was like a missionary, it was easy for them. Grandma Eran was a very religious woman. She gave Mama guidance in supporting her husband, participating in church and community activities, and having a sense of self and being a good homemaker. Mama was the president of the Home Mission Society for years. She was brought up in the church also. Her father was a Methodist minister. Grandma would teach the other women to be responsible, to be a strong force and get more done. They had officers within: president, secretary, and treasurer.

Since all the women were farm wives and had to take care of their families first, the needs of the community were left up to whoever was able to get away at that particular time. Sometimes their own families would have to wait, if something else was more important. I remember Mama had Jimmy and me go with her one time to a woman's house, and we swept the yard. There was no grass in that area, and very few leaves and twigs. Jimmy and I laughed about it, because we were just sweeping dirt. We swept the inside of the house real good, and mopped the wooden floors.

Many women from other churches who were members of the Home Mission Society came out to our church, First Hopewell, to share in fellowship, and carry back to their communities what they learned from ours. They all knew Grandma and the extent of her involvement. It was a privilege to them. Grandma would have two days of meetings and prayer service and give her teachings about what the Home Mission Society was all about.

One time, two women from a church on the other side of Columbia came out and stayed with us for two nights. Before they came, we scrubbed the floor, made sure no spiderwebs were on the walls, wiped off the chest and dresser, put clean doilies on them, and changed the sheets. Everything had to be clean. At the house, they'd sit around with Mama and talk about things Grandma had done and what Mama did in our community. They were pleasant and dressed well. They slept in the back bedroom off the dining room. We had the old Victrola on top of the chest in that room and would go in and put on a record when the women were talking to Mama on the front porch or in the kitchen when Mama was cooking.

One of Mama's brothers, Uncle Tobie (Gilbert), was a Holiness preacher in downtown Columbia. His church would be packed with folks. When we went down there, it was like going to a party. I never saw so much dancing and singing — dancing between seats, all in the aisles, and along the walls in the back of the church. They had more Holy Spirit than anybody I ever saw, I figured, looking around at all the different people up and being a part of the celebrating and praising the Lord. It was just a few women scattered about in our church shouting during the sermon.

One of my classmates would shout in our church, and she was young. We were all outdone, because we were the same age and never felt the spirit that way. But in Uncle Tobie's church, it was the whole congregation up and moving. It was mesmerizing watching them — arms flopping about above their heads, shoulders and upper bodies shaking and shuddering, big hips gyrating from side to side, whole bodies moved by stomping feet. It was quite a sight. Uncle Tobie always wore his black suit, sparkling white shirt and skinny black bow tie, with a handkerchief and fountain pen in his lapel pocket. He was tall with snow-white hair. He looked important. Those big, round-rim glasses saw everything.

The Other Events

Funerals were the other single biggest social event that took place at church. They were bigger than revival Sunday, especially if you were well-known, because they reached churches and communities everywhere.

One of my first cousins, Alvernell, was one of Aunt Sarah's (Sang's) daughters and lived in Detroit. When she died in February of 1945, she was brought back home to be buried. We were told she died of natural causes. What I remember about her funeral is going over to Aunt Sang's and Uncle Hark's house with Mama. I remember the front porch being packed with people — all over the yard and all over the house. Alvernell's coffin was in the living room of Aunt Sang's house because this was where the wake was being held. Everybody in the community was there. Most of the people, myself included, had never seen an open casket, one that was open all the way down to the feet. Alvernell had on a blue gown, with a little white fur on top, and matching blue slippers. It was hard to believe that she was dead because she looked so pretty. She looked like she was just sleeping. Food was everywhere, and people walked all over the house, eating and talking quietly.

Not long after Alvernell died, Grandpa up and died on June 17,

1945, when I was six years old. It was of natural causes; he was seventy-seven years old. I don't remember him being sick, either. Tootsie thinks he died of heart trouble. All I remember is that I went out to the barn, sat on the wooden fence, and cried and cried. Mama and Papa were too busy seeing after Grandma and making arrangements for the funeral to notice. Dan came out and got me.

Mama told us, "Your grandpa was old, and he had a bad heart." I didn't know what "having a bad heart" was, but I did know that when you got old, that's when you died. I don't remember his funeral much, but I do remember that on the same day that they buried Grandpa, I cried and cried in the morning, and by the afternoon, I was playing.

Death became more real to me when a neighborhood boy drowned in a pond. He was young. He and a friend of his were crossing the pond on a horse. He must have gotten a cramp and fallen off the horse, because his friend said that he thought he was right behind him, but when he looked back, he wasn't. The horse came out, but the boy was lost in the water. Although they found his body, it was too late to save him. Now I remember how I felt about that. It made me realize that someone my age could die. I knew I did not want to die young, so it was very scary for me to think that you could.

"Her Price Is Far Above Rubies"

My mind's eye is filled with countless images of Grandma Eran — her bright smile, or carrying a bucket full of spring water in each hand and a jug on her head, or one of her big, wet kisses waiting to happen just before she planted it on your cheek. Any way you looked at it, Grandma was goodness incarnate, and when I saw her perched up on her big high-backed armchair decorated with white paper flowers as if it was a throne before God, I thought she was the Queen of Heaven — not my grandmother, but Jesus' grandmother, holy as holy could be.

This was on her Appreciation Day, a special service dedicated to her on one of our third-Sunday meetings at church. There sat Grandma

Eran, as if she belonged in a tiara and ermine cape, but wearing her usual long, white dress with layers of lace over the cotton fabric, and white tie shoes, white gloves, and a small, white hat with white net hanging over one side of her face. She pulled up her veil so as to see all the people in the church and thank them personally as they walked by her, and every now and then she wiped away a tear with her white handkerchief. Now an outsider would no doubt find it all a bit much, but for anyone present, and also for anyone who knew her far and wide, Grandma was for real. The adoration was warranted and it was genuine — in praise of her many years of fellowship with God, leadership in the community, missionary work throughout Marion County, and moral guidance for so many women.

"Her candle goeth not out by night.... She reacheth forth her hands to the needy.... Strength and honor are her clothing.... In her tongue is the law of kindness.... She eateth not the bread of idleness," rang the voice of the Rev. Lumzy. "Many daughters have done virtuously, but thou excellest them all. Give her of the fruit of her hands; and let her own works praise her in the gates!" At this point, in his excerpts from the Proverbs, the Rev. Lumzy called the congregation forth to pin their gifts upon Grandma's dress and it was soon covered with bills of money. The choir sang "Holy, Holy, Holy" and "Have Thine Own Way" and other songs that rang of strength and commitment.

Grandma was president of the Home Mission Society of the East Pearl River District for thirty-five years. For decades, when other women from the surrounding communities ran against her for the office, they lost. Even when they banded together to launch a campaign, she was victorious. "It takes grit, grace, and greenbacks to be over people," she used to say. "A lot of people think the church is supposed to put out the money, but what they don't know is you have to put out money yourself to keep things running. You have to stand up for what you believe and put your money behind it, and you can't back down from anybody."

Grandma did more than lead the way. She taught and trained the women. She had her own strengths: she knew the Bible and she knew people. But most of all, she knew how to teach them — by being a model herself. She never drank or cursed. She never fell to lust or revenge, gossip or jealousy. She taught the younger women in the church by example. Many of these women got up to give a little talk about her in front of the church. And when it was all over and hands clapped and feet tapped as the singing started, Grandma sang right along. She went home that Sunday in a state of totally uplifted grace.

Grandma died when I was fourteen years old, in 1953, and that feels like yesterday. Papa and Uncle Luther sat at her bedside with their heads bowed, not saying a word. We were all lined up against the wall, just looking. Mama and Aunt Pearlie were crying softly. It seemed like that went on forever. She was like some person in the Bible, or someone you read about in the news.

A lot of people came to funerals where they did not really know the person who died but knew someone who was familiar with the deceased. Grandma Eran's funeral was such. It was crowded, with standing all around and outside. As president of the Home Mission Society for thirty-five years, she was a leader and taught so many others — women who became presidents in their own church. Her influence stretched far and wide.

There was a procession, marching around to view the body. The sisters had a banner from their particular churches and the different church groups marched together. It was entertaining, but a sadness hung over the congregation. The people cried softly, patting their eyes with perfumed handkerchiefs. Everyone, it seemed, was dressed in either black or white, but the hats, shoes, and bags were all very stylish. The hats were swaying in all the right directions that day.

The baskets of fresh strawberries or the big tea cakes from Grandma would be no more. There would be no more spending the night up at Grandma's, or listening to her quietly talking to Grandpa, or glancing at him without saying a word when he got carried away with his talks. Grandma and Grandpa were our extensions of Mama and Papa. Having them was like having another set of parents.

Hold Your Breath

By the time I was twelve years old and listening to the adults in church, I believed that if I didn't get baptized, I was going to die and go straight to Hell very soon. So, the big day came when it was to happen. There was a full, fresh body of water called "Little River" that ran under the bridge about a hundred and fifty feet just down the road from the church house. The embankment on one side of the river was just level enough in places, with a bumpy walkway down to the water. The bank was green with grass that was, I'm sure, cut by one of the deacons for the baptism. Anticipating this event caused a little nervousness in me because I could not swim. How I wished I could have waited longer to join the church in the first place. Then I wouldn't have had to be going through this.

There were three other girls with me that special day. It was late August and hot as all get out. The water would probably be warm. Mama took me into the conference room behind the pulpit, where I changed into a long, white dress with a white slip. It was pretty, but not pretty enough to make me feel good about the water. The other girls were changing, too, with their mamas. We all loaded up in the back of Papa's pickup truck and he drove us down to the river's edge. The Rev. Lumzy, our pastor, was already standing in the water. If he had sported a beard, he would have looked like Jesus Christ. Mama, the other mamas, and Benny Thornton were standing on the riverbank.

We all jumped out of the truck. The Rev. Lumzy had on a white smock. He told us the water was not deep, but it came up to his knees. That was too deep for me. We lined up and waited until Benny Thornton read a selection from the scriptures and the Rev. Lumzy read something. I was not listening at all, waiting for him to call my name.

"Mary, I'm scared," I said to one of the girls. "I don't know how to swim."

"You don't have to," she said. "Just hold your breath a long time

124

when you go under. He'll bring you up real fast. It'll all be over before you know it and you can breathe."

I was first in line. "Oh, Lordy, here I go."

The Reverend called me. "Come over here, Charlene, by me."

I took a few steps in the water, reaching for his outstretched hand. I didn't want to let go of it. He pulled me toward him, put his right hand behind my back between my shoulders, and down I went, stiff as a board. He told me not to be scared, but I didn't hear that.

"I baptize you in the name of the Father, the Son, and the Holy Ghost." Once I felt the water, my mouth just flew open and filled up with it. The Rev. Lumzy had me standing up just in time to choke, cough, and gasp out all that water. I was never so scared. I thought I was going to drown. As I was coming out of the water, Mama had a big towel she patted on me, and then we all climbed into the back of Papa's truck again and rode up to the church house. Getting out of those wet clothes was a godsend.

As I've already mentioned, Papa was a deacon in the church and Mama was president of the Home Mission Society. Being a pillar of the community, Papa was respected by whites and colored people. He was fair to people and worked hard and stood up for what was right. Mama was as strong as Papa in her ability to stand up for what she believed in. She didn't back down to anybody.

Papa was a big farmer revered by both blacks and whites in the community for his masonry and carpentry as well. Because he had so many children, he took his service to the church and schools as seriously as he did his farming and everything else. Luther was a small farmer who never built wood homes or laid bricks or raised a big family, but lived as a bachelor into his late thirties. Known far and wide for his dapper dressing and genuine good looks, Luther had another kind of reputation. His real treat for my brothers was to take them downtown to make the rounds with the music and the girls, and he was beloved for his boy-talk and man-talk with all of them. After all, Clifford, Tootsie, and Boy Noah had their own car and had tales to tell

Luther about their house party escapades. Luther's game was people, charm, and attention — and maybe all this was his way of holding his own next to Papa, the pillar of the community on so many counts.

The new pastors came and went and things went on as usual for years. Some were there for a long time and others weren't. Some could preach well and others could not. It seemed the old dependables who did the real caring for the community and its members were slowly vanishing. Their influence was not nearly as strong among the people as it had been. Respect for the leaders was not the same.

Think of how slave labor helped build churches, and slaves worshipped with their masters before the Civil War. Some were buried in the same graveyards as their masters. When the white churches got too crowded with the growing congregation, they sold their little churches to the Negroes and they had their own worship service, separate from their masters. So the churches were separate for as long as racism existed, and segregation so ever-present. The church was a stabilizing force for us country folks. It had more influence over the people than anything else. When anything went wrong or folks had problems, they always came back to the church. Many of them felt the Lord would take care of all their problems when something happened. It was said by many, "It's the Lord's will."

Chapter 6

School Days

One day at the end of my sixth grade class, my teacher had us fill out a form with a lot of questions on it. They were questions about the number of brothers and sisters, their ages, which ones lived at home or were away at college, and how much land Papa and Grandpa Daniel had. I never thought much about Papa's land; all I knew was that we picked cotton in a lot of big fields in four different places and corn and potatoes in other places.

When I got home that day, I went out to the barn where Papa was working and asked him about the land. The other answers I knew. That was the first time I learned that the school and the shop across the road were built on Grandpa's land and that the land where Grandpa's old house stood was on land Grandpa owned. Because of the questions, I thought about other families in our neighborhood that had their own farms. I never knew exactly why we had to fill out that form.

Our school was a little bigger than most of the other small schools. Blue Springs, Bassfield and Rose Hill would all eventually become consolidated. Within two or three miles from our school were the Lee and Watts schools. The community leaders and parents got together and decided the two smaller schools should be consolidated with ours. The number of students and grade levels were considered along with the better teachers and principals of the schools. There was a lot of bickering and resentment that went on; physical blows took place at a couple of the meetings. It was all everybody talked about. Consolidation was eventually agreed on and the schools were renamed La Marion High. It went only to the eleventh grade. All the Marion County students went to the Columbia colored school to finish twelfth grade, and so all my older brothers went there. The Lamar County line was nearby, and the Watts students went to Sumrall to finish the twelfth grade.

None of the colored schools were in good shape: supplies were low, and textbooks were the used throwaways from the white Improve High School. The pay was bad and good teachers were hard to come by. Professor White was the principal from the 1930s through 1946. He was good and had a sister-in-law, Miss Riley, who was one of the best teachers La Marion ever had. During the latter part of 1946, Professor Alexander was principal for a short time, and Professor Coleman finished his term. Before Alexander left, he got a lot of typewriters from the Improve High School. Never having had typewriters before, the students were all excited. Learning to type was going to be the thing. Just as the excitement built to a high, it was crushed because the typewriters were all taken back. The letdown was felt by students and teachers alike.

Professor Price came to La Marion in 1947 and things started to get better. He improved the overall condition of the schools and the teachers improved. They were almost all college graduates. The community folks and parents of the students all liked Professor Price. He even got a few of the typewriters back. Why had they been taken?

Two houses were on the grounds. One single-family house was for the principal and his family. The other house across the schoolyard had two sections. On one side was a bedroom unit for a married teacher, and on the other side were three single rooms for three single female teachers, with a small kitchen and a bath. The other married teachers lived out in the community and a few in downtown Columbia. One single male math teacher lived with a family nearby. He was a good teacher, a dapper dresser and good-looking. I think all the girls had a crush on him.

Some of the female teachers were not much older than the oldest boys in school, especially if the boys were behind a year or two during their early years. To make up for the attraction, the outside young men — army boys on furlough — caught their eye. Some courting was going on, but it was not all out in the open. My brother Clifford, in the army, would come home on furlough. Every time after he left, Jimmy and I would get a big, red apple in school from not one but two of the prettiest teachers. We may not have been in their particular class, but we saw these teachers every day. Other times, one of them would happen to come down to the house to sit and talk with Mama. I just thought they liked Mama and Papa. It made me feel good because they were real friendly to us at school.

Clifford would only say, "You all have some pretty schoolteachers, and they're smart, too." They wore pretty clothes, high-heeled shoes, hair all curled, and some wore lipstick. One or two plain Janes wore granny dresses and old-fashioned, low-heeled shoes. Their hair would be pulled back into a little ball in the back. They were all good teachers, though.

Our schoolhouse was shaped like a big H and was made of cement blocks outside and a lot of wood inside. The auditorium was in the center with the front entrance facing west. Across the front was a patio that had two inside rooms; on the right side was the principal's office, and on the left was the math classroom. Three rooms were across the south side, the fourth, fifth (center stage), sixth grades, and across the north side were the science, English, and home economics classrooms. Tall windows ran across all the rooms and the whole length of the auditorium.

The elementary building was separate and out back on the side. It had three rooms—first through third grade classrooms. It was made of wood and painted white. All the rooms were very bright. A three-seater girls' toilet was located not too far from the elementary building, and the boys' toilet was across the back playground. The playground in back was a few acres of land, open land for a lot of students to run and play. All the furniture — teachers' desks, students' desks, chairs, and even the floors— were made of wood.

The front yard of the main building was a playground with a basketball court. To the left of the main building was a lunchroom, with the first half a big room used for canning and storage and the second half for cooking and eating. It had at least four long tables that could seat fifteen to twenty students at one time, as well as three small tables that seated five, which were used by the teachers when they ate lunch.

Papa was as active in the PTA (Parent Teacher Association) as he was in the church, and it became clearer to me when I was in secondary and high school how active he was. He was on the school board. He had a say about how the school was run and the qualifications of teachers and principals. His opinion was respected throughout the community because people knew him to be fair and honest. It was not unusual for some folks in the community to come to Papa when they had certain kinds of problems. He could talk for people, just as he did within the church. A couple of my nieces were surprised to see Papa's signature on their diplomas.

My first day of preschool, Carzella took me to Ms. Cagins' classroom. She was my teacher. I started crying and Ms. Cagins could not stop me, so finally she sent one of the other students to go out and get Carzella to come and talk to me. I just wanted to go home to Mama. When I saw Carzella in the doorway, I calmed down. Here was my sister. Carzella came over, knelt down beside me, and wiped my face with the tail of her dress. Then she told me to stop crying and that I would be able to play with my little friends at recess. When she started to talk to me, I was able to look around the classroom and realized that there were children I knew from visiting their houses and them visiting mine. I had been too upset to see any of them. So I quieted down.

But as soon as the bell rang for recess, I was looking for Carzella. She found me in the schoolyard and she had two of my little friends with her, Fanny Mae and Frances. They walked up to me and started to play. They had been right in the classroom all that time. When we went back to class, I sat next to Fannie Mae. I looked forward to recess after that because not only was I with my friends, I was also going to play games. At recess, we played "Little Sally Walker," which is a song from the black musical tradition. It was played by a group of us, at least six, all holding hands in a circle. One child was selected by the group to "sit in the saucer," which meant sitting on the ground in the middle of the circle. When it was my turn the group began to march around me in a circle, singing "Little Sally Walker":

> *Little Sally Walker, sittin' in a saucer,*
> *She weepin', she whinin',*
> *she swallowed a glass of water.*
> *Rise, Sally, rise,*
> *Wipe your weepin' eyes,*
> *Put your hands on your hips,*
> *And let your backbone slip.*
> *Oh, shake it to the east,*
> *Oh, shake it to the west*
> *Oh, shake it to the one that you love the best!*

Another fun game was "Here We Go 'Round the Mulberry Bush." That consisted of singing and motioning, also. There were many other songs we sang and games we played at school and at home when we were visited by our friends and when we visited their homes. We played jump rope, we shot marbles, and we played pop the whip, in which 15 or more kids were needed to make it really good — the more, the better. We all held hands and ran as fast as we could for about seventy-five feet. The first ten or so kids would be able to stop, but the ones on the end of the line had built up a lot of momentum so that it was difficult for them to stop without falling or losing their grip on those next to them. Usually, the last two or three who lost their grip also fell. This was when the whip was "popped." It could be dangerous for those who couldn't run fast — and running fast was the key; you had to remain upright and intact with the person next to you. We also sang songs like "Pick a Bale of Cotton," "London Bridge," "Mary Had a Little Lamb," and "Rock-a-bye Baby."

The elementary school children were let out earlier, at about 11:30

so that they could eat first, and the other grades later. The girls' basketball team practiced for thirty to forty-five minutes, and then they ate between 12:00 to 12:30. The boys practiced basketball sometimes across the road where the shop building was located. While many of the students watched them practice, they also ate around 12:30 to 1:00. At least ten to fifteen boys practiced, and eventually, everybody got to eat.

We entered the lunchroom through the back section, walking through the storage and canning area. Then, all we had to do was walk up four steps into the cafeteria-style serving area. Mrs. Lee would fill up our plates with two green vegetables that could have been anything from sweet peas to green beans, collard greens or turnips, maybe sweet corn or mashed potatoes, sweet potatoes, beets, cornbread, or fried sweet corn. For dessert, there was some sort of wonderful apple, peach, blueberry, blackberry, or pecan pie that she would serve along with cold milk. It was always a treat.

The lunchroom could seat eighty to a hundred students at a time. Lunchtime was fun — everybody was busy finding seats with their buddies and playmates. As soon as school was out, Carzella came and got me, along with Celestine, Myrtis, Paul, and Dan. Then we all walked home together, and that became the routine. There were no school buses at that time, so we had to walk about a quarter of a mile to and from school.

It would be three years later, when I was in the third grade, that we got a yellow school bus. Cousin Glossie was the school bus driver. He would honk his horn for us to come out to the road by the time he got to our stop. When we heard that horn, it was like a war zone in the house. One or two of us were in the kitchen — Darlene and I, with Jimmy and Myrtis up front in the bathroom mirror putting on final touches for the day.

Papa would be sitting at the kitchen fireplace before we left, drinking coffee, and Mama was in the kitchen cleaning up from breakfast. I was rushing to get my books and my sweater while trying to finish eating my breakfast, and then brushing my teeth. It seemed like we never had enough time to get ready so that we could be waiting outside when the bus came. We always scrambled to get out to the road on time, though. Mama used to say, "I told you all to get up earlier so you can be ready," and Papa would say, "I told you all to get up earlier so you can be ready." He would sit there and drink his coffee and shake his head in amazement at how we got so excited when we heard that horn honking. He always gave each of us fifteen cents for lunch money. Cousin Glossie, I'm sure, left a little earlier because he knew we would probably be a little late. But we always made it to school on time.

The first through fourth grades were fairly routine: playing in the schoolyard at recess, looking out the window during class, passing notes while in class. And in fifth grade there would be looking at dirty pictures of half-naked women on cards that one of the boys in class had and was always trying to hide from the teacher. All the students were trying to look, and most of us did, eyes wide open and mouths open, too.

My fifth grade year was also the worst of all. One day about the time school ended, at about three o'clock, my menstrual period started in the classroom. It was not my first period. When I stood up, a spot was on the back of my skirt. With tears in my eyes, I sat back down and waited until all the other students left the classroom and then walked up to the teacher — a male teacher of all things. I told him I had a spot on my dress and he spoke softly to me, took out a safety pin from his desk drawer, folded my skirt over the spot and told me to go on home.

Things started to get more interesting by sixth grade because the little boys started to notice me and be playful toward me. They'd say funny things to make me laugh, tell me how I looked, or ask me to help them with their homework. Never taking any of them seriously, I would make fun of them with my little friends. My mind couldn't be farther away from their lessons.

One day in class, I gave in to temptation and did exactly what one of my classmates asked me to do. It all had to do with sneaking a piece of hard candy into my mouth. Jawbreakers were very hard, quarter-size, round pieces of multicolored candy to suck on. It was probably bad for my teeth, but when my friend gave me one in Miss Magee's class, I took it. Talking and sucking on it all at the same time, it tasted good and sweet. The only problem was it got stuck in my throat. Mouth open wide, eyes big, I clutched my throat and stumbled toward Miss Magee. She calmly walked over and hit me between my shoulders, up high real hard, and that jawbreaker flew out of my mouth. Never again did I do anything in class I wasn't supposed to do, remembering what the Reverend Lumzy said about getting into trouble.

Myrtis drove the car when Papa would let her, and because I already knew how to drive the tractor and the pickup truck, I was just waiting to drive a car, especially Paul's and Dan's car. Paul taught all of us to drive, and I was eager to learn. Dan and Paul took us to everything that wasn't related to going to church. Papa had bought them a car, just as he did brother Tootsie and Boy Noah, because he got tired of them using his car.

Going to Town

We could go anywhere with Dan and Paul. Papa and Mama didn't ask any questions. They'd drop us off at the picture show and we'd sit there and watch —first, a main feature, and then some cliff-hanger series. We'd watch from the beginning to the end. We were rarely out past ten or eleven o'clock at night, and somehow Mama and Papa would always be awake when we got home. Going downtown was the thing to do. It was a social event. It seemed special, maybe because we were in the fields every day working. Going downtown started with taking a bath and putting on some nice school clothes. We walked around, down one sidewalk and up the other, meeting up with friends from school, laughing and talking, buying hotdogs, hamburgers, and Cokes or snowballs or ice cream cones at the Dairy Freeze stand. It was like a ritual, and I enjoyed every minute of it.

Columbia was so alive then. It had a lumber mill, a navy store, a large manufacturing plant that made hosiery and clothes, a canning plant, and other stuff. On the weekends, especially, the population grew from the six thousand who actually lived there to hundreds more. The town was bustling with movement everywhere: Noise, whistles blowing, people calling out and waving. The people wore overalls, Levis, khaki for a few. The courthouse square was lined up with old men, colored and white, spitting tobacco juice and blowing cigarette smoke.

Old cars and trucks were parked everywhere. If someone's children or relatives from Chicago, Los Angeles, or New York were home to visit, everybody knew about it and couldn't wait to see what kind of big, black, shiny car they had. They'd park it right by the courthouse so everybody could see it; they always came downtown. The men would be dressed up, with long, black, shiny shoes, a black suit and white shirt and black tie. The driver would put his jacket on after he got out of the car. We'd all be looking. The father of one of my sister-in-laws, from California, especially, his image stays in my mind. He drove a long, black Cadillac every time he came back to Mississippi, and I thought he must be rich with that big car and always in a suit. He didn't pick cotton like we did.

The white folks from out in the country whom we knew would always speak to us. Everybody seemed to know Papa. At the time, it was as if more white folks knew him than colored people in the communities. I never moved off the sidewalk when passing a white person on the streets or hold my head down. We went in and out of every store and I spent my money mostly at the ten-cent store. We could buy a lot of things, a little plastic ring or bracelet. No earrings or lipstick because Mama didn't allow us to wear lipstick. Maybe a little bow for my hair but no fingernail polish, either. It was the going to town, the excitement at the end of the week we looked forward to every weekend. If Papa didn't want to let us go, I'd bargain with him, telling him how hard we worked during the week. I didn't see any reason why we could not go. He gave in most of the time.

On Saturday afternoons when we didn't go downtown we had our own good times at home. Dan had taught all of us to jitterbug and swing dance. Myrtis would get on that piano and play more boogie-woogie than we had ever heard. Jimmy and I would cut loose with Dan in the living room and out on the front porch. Darlene would be in the swing, swinging, and Paul would be doing the slow drag, while the rest of us were all over the place. When Jimmy took over the playing, her boogie-woogie sounded better than Myrtis's. Hers was like the phonograph recorders. My playing was all by ear, and I didn't get between Myrtis's and Jimmy's playing. Mama and Papa would be visiting the sick and shut-ins and weren't at home during our dance sessions.

One night, a loud knock on the front door woke all of us up. It was the middle of the week, and we had to go to school the next day. Papa got up first and switched on the porch light asking, "Who is it?" Whoever it was kept knocking. By this time, we were all up looking out the window onto the front porch. Paul went up front from his room to where Papa was just opening the front door. A white man was standing there shaking his head from side to side. He told Papa that Dan and Herbert (a cousin) had been involved in an accident down on Highway 24 by Hilltop Grocery. They hit a mule that was crossing the road. They didn't get hurt, but the mule was killed and the pickup truck was torn up. The man who lived nearby heard the noise, and once he saw they were not hurt, he drove them home. Papa was so thankful to the man and that they were not hurt. We all were, and went back to bed. Papa didn't fuss at them at all.

Ballgames

Our school had an outstanding basketball team. They won the playoffs in the NFA (New Farmers of America) in 1952 and 1953. They won tournaments because they were just good. Professor Steel was impressed with Dan, Paul, and Robert because our white neighbor,

Charley Harris (a championship winner for three years for Sumrall, Mississippi High), taught them moves and maneuvers on the court they had never seen before. After school, they could be found playing in Charley's backyard, down the road from our house. All the colored schools went down to Lampton High gym for games, competitions, and tournaments. It was the biggest in the whole area for colored students. The ballgames meant everything to every young boy growing up out in the country. They'd rather play ball than eat. Dan, Paul, Robert, Harvey, John Edward, J.C., Joe, and other good players, it was their life. They played all colored schools—Lampton, Columbia, Pine Grove, Hub Academy and Friendship. One year they went outside Marion County up to Utica Institute in Northern, Mississippi, on their turf. There were some problems with the referee and the scoring as to which team actually won.

Cousin Glossie drove the students to all the games and after they were over, he would drop some of them off on Highway 24 at a neighbor's house, who would then drive them home. There were too many little dirt or gravel roads to go down for the school bus. Papa would have Dan and Paul dropped off at Albert Jackson's house.

Dan and Paul took us out to Hattiesburg a few times to see a game at Rowan High School. One time, we saw the Harlem Globetrotters. That was the night of all nights. It was like watching a dance group on stage. They could do anything on the floor and up in the air with their bodies and the basketball. They talked and made fun, all the while playing basketball. It was something none of us had ever seen in all of Hattiesburg.

Paul was as good in baseball as he was in basketball. He got invited down to Florida for the baseball tryouts his last year in high school. Papa didn't think too much of basketball or baseball as a profession and didn't want him to go—and Paul didn't, but he wanted to. In the meantime, a white man we knew wanted colored and whites to get together, especially since the young colored boys were being drafted into the army. Dan, Paul, Robert, and two girls from Second Hopewell integrated the Old Rocky Branch Church in 1951. They had no problems.

Everything changed in 1952. Dan graduated high school and went to Alcorn College for a short time. He was drafted into the army in June 1953. The morning he left, I was standing in my bedroom window looking out to the backyard. Paul was waiting at Papa's pickup truck for someone to drive him to downtown Columbia to the Greyhound bus station. All the draftees met there and were driven up to Jackson, Mississippi, before heading to Ft. Lewis, Washington. Dan served two years. While there, he played basketball and got a basketball scholarship at St. Martin's College in Olympia, Washington. He played basketball and baseball there for three years. Paul said it may have been due to the white girls at the college (segregation) that he left. He returned home in 1958, my last year of high school, and got back into what he knew — brick masonry.

Almost a year after Dan's drafting, Paul got drafted. He went and visited my brother Bufford in San Francisco, California, for a few weeks (Dan did the same before he went in). Beginning December 8 or 9, 1953, Paul was stationed at Ft. Ord, California, Ft. Knox, Kentucky, and Ft. Hood, all for two years. Bufford had served but was called back about six months after Paul and went to Ft. Lewis also. Along with a cousin, Foster, all were stationed at Ft. Lewis.

With Dan and Paul away in the service in 1953, Myrtis was the oldest at home and the activity around the house was cut down a lot. She could drive, and we would still go everywhere, but not as much. With school and church activities, our social life continued. The yellow school bus was always in sight. Chores and chores all the time. I loved to cut the grass, and there was a lot of grass to cut around the house. Uncle Willis, Aunt Roxie's husband, still occasionally came out to the farm and cut our grass with his power lawnmower, as he had done years earlier. When Papa got a gas-powered lawnmower it was a big relief, because not only was it easier and faster to use, it did a much better job than the manual one. The yard looked so much prettier with all the grass evenly cut.

The very same year, 1953, when Dan and Paul were drafted (June and December), Grandma Eran died in May. That's one year that just didn't go too well. Grandma was like a pillar — a strong leader in our community. We wouldn't have her anymore to stay all night with, or to walk down the back woods behind her house to get spring water or juicy strawberries; or to see her at the top of the hill walking down to our house. Her dying was worse than Dan and Paul going into the army.

4-H Club

Seventh grade was very important to me. Mama let me go to a 4-H Club girls' camp in Jackson. This was the first time I had ever been away from home with friends from school. The camp session was five days long, starting on a Tuesday. Five of us from La Marion School were driven to downtown Columbia by Cousin Glossie. There, we met other 4-H Club members from at least four other schools. We were loaded onto a big school bus and driven to the campsite, which was just outside Jackson, and we arrived at mid-afternoon. Once there, we were split off from the original groups of students with whom we had arrived and then matched up with others according to our ages. We shared quarters with girls up to two years older or younger than we were. Our living quarters consisted of a small, cabin-like building with four bunk beds in each. There were folded linens at the head of each bed — two sheets, a light spread, and a pillowcase. The first thing we did was to choose our beds and make them up. I took the top one and climbed the small ladder to bounce on the bed. There was a small dresser in a space between the head and foot for each set of beds, a small table, and two very small closets for hanging our clothes.

A camp counselor came by and stuck her head in the door to tell everyone to be in the recreation room in fifteen minutes. We did some fast unpacking and got out of there. Unpacking was fun, because I had a couple of new summer outfits — blue shorts and a white top, and also a pinafore yellow dress. Everything else was old, but those girls had never seen my clothes, so they didn't know what was new or old. I had my little personals: toothbrush and toothpaste, Chapstick (because I was too young to wear lipstick), fingernail polish, comb, brush, a bar of Ivory soap with a soap dish, a small plastic container of hand lotion, and deodorant.

The "Rec Room" was in the big main building located at the center of the campgrounds. Signs and arrows pointed the way. All the other children were there. When everyone was gathered, they began to give us general instructions about the camp, which included an introduction of the staff and an orientation to the cafeteria, the bathrooms, the dock, and the big area that had been partitioned off for swimming. The Rec Room was where all kinds of activities took place. This was the designated space for making things such as candles, jewelry boxes, mirrors, pot holders, picture frames, plant boxes, belts, strings of beads, and just about everything. Also, the Rec Room was where everybody was to meet every morning to be told what the activities of the day and the evening were to be.

The remainder of the first day was devoted to walking around the grounds to meet other students. With the freedom to wander around, we eventually ran into our friends from our own school. We had the liberty that day of going for short walks just so we could become familiar with the surroundings. That night, we all gathered in the Rec Room for a more formal welcome by the staff. During the day, the staff wore shorts, but in the evening, they all wore dresses. We never had an opportunity to change between activities, so we were all wearing the same clothes we arrived in earlier that afternoon. At a little reception, we were served snacks, small sandwiches and soft drinks. This lasted for about an hour, and when it was over, we all went back to our bunks for the night.

The next morning, we gathered in the Rec Room once again where there were various "how to" areas— arts and crafts stands with instructors or counselors who taught specific classes. I chose the jewelry box area. The teacher had all the materials laid out, and all we had to do was to nail the pieces of wood together. The boxes were all different sizes and shapes. We had to match up the pieces. This was different from our shop class at school, where we were instructed by the teacher as to how to cut all the pieces of wood, sand them down, and then nail them together and stain them; but it was still interesting.

That night, we went to a talent show put on by our counselors because on the fourth night we would have to put on our own talent show. The counselors put on their short skits, sang ragtime, played the piano, and read poetry. It was a lot of fun watching them perform. This prepared us so that when our turn came we would feel more comfortable. We wouldn't be embarrassed to get up in front of a large group of people and perform. Their example worked.

On the second day, we all went either swimming or hiking with a guide. I went hiking. So did one of my friends from school and a lot of the other children. It was pretty early in the morning when we started out, which was long before it got hot later in the morning. Around the campsite, there were a lot of trees that provided shade, but during midday, even in the shade, it was hot, maybe 80 degrees. The hike lasted about two hours, with the guide pointing out all the interesting flowers, trees, and insects along the way.

We were always allowed to swim before lunch, and that was the only time I wished that I knew how, or felt that not knowing caused an awkward moment in my life. It was the only time that I felt inadequate. There were other girls sitting alongside me with their feet dangling in the water or splashing about. They didn't know how to swim, either. We were all happy just playing in the water. Even so, I hated the idea that I didn't know how to swim. The kids swimming looked as though they were having so much fun, diving under the water and coming up again. They seemed to be enjoying themselves so much more.

Later that day was a softball game. The coach selected the teams randomly, placing one or two of the tallest children on each team. My team won because we had better players and pure luck, I guess. But it was easy for me, because I already knew how to play softball and so did a few of the others on my team. That night, all the students gathered in the Rec Room. We couldn't wait to see what they had planned for us next. Maybe we would learn to make something else. This time, all the arts and crafts materials were laid out alongside the instructions and the counselors were on hand to assist us. There was a small section of the Rec Room that was set up as a library, with a few chairs in one corner and all kinds of books— English books and history books, a few novels, like *Rip Van Winkle,* and a set of *World Book* encyclopedias. That section was relaxing.

On the third day of camp, there was a big picnic that started at two o'clock out on the grounds. All the tables were covered with food — pies, cakes, sandwiches, potato chips— and two of the counselors were cooking hot dogs and hamburgers on a grill. Everybody was out in their T-shirts, shorts, and sneakers with white socks, and we were all anxious to eat. It was festive. There was as much food as we could eat. The hot dogs and hamburgers just kept filling up that big platter on the table along with more and more ketchup and mustard, onion, radishes, pickles, and sliced tomatoes that were kept in bowls. The soft drinks— grape, orange, strawberry, and 7-Up — were in a big barrel of ice to keep cold.

I ate as much as I could without getting a stomachache, and I had a great time. The picnic lasted until all the food was gone, which was around six that evening. The only thing I could do after that was lie down and never get up, but at seven that same evening our talent show would be starting. So it meant getting back to our bunks, having a shower, and going over to the Rec Room.

Earlier that morning, one of the counselors had gotten a list of all the talent acts that would be performed, and a program was made out for the evening. It started with a song by the whole group, "Row Your Boat." One group started, and another joined in seconds later on cue. We sang in rounds with four groups in all. It was a lot of fun. The next act was a poem by one of the girls. Then a group sang "Old MacDonald Had a Farm." The third act was a dance by Bevelyn Charlene Exposé. I had learned a dance earlier that day and one of my friends played the piano. It was three or four different basic steps. I already knew most of them, but I just kept practicing them to the music.

Performing in the talent show reminded me of when I was younger, about seven years old, and I used to stand up to recite a verse from the Bible in front of everybody sitting in church. I would get about halfway through the verse and start crying, with everyone looking at me. By now, I had lost my stage fright and could get up and speak or recite before a large group. So my dance number at the talent show went well all the way. I wasn't scared a bit.

The fourth act was another reading by a student, and this was followed by a group song. At the end, we all sang "Deep in the Heart of Texas." There was voting by the counselors for each category: Most Popular, Most Talented, Miss Charm, and Most Likely to Succeed. I was voted Miss Charm and given a plaque at the end of the program that I cherished for years to come. Each girl had to present the object she had made in arts and crafts to the whole group. All the counselors were present, as were the few men who served as coaches, along with the two gardeners whom we saw every day tending the grounds.

The whole five days had been full and entertaining and fun. The next day, which was Saturday, was a little sad because we all had to say our good-byes and load up onto the various yellow school buses to be driven back to our hometowns and farms. We left at about ten o'clock that Saturday morning and arrived in Columbia at about one o'clock. When we got there, Cousin Glossie was waiting out by the courthouse where he had dropped us off on Tuesday. We were glad to be back home but sad to leave the camp because it was such a new experience and such a fun thing to do, being away from home for the first time. We had something to talk about for months. We had to give a report to the class the next week. I showed my Miss Charm plaque to the class and felt very special at school. I also felt like I was really growing up now, because Mama had let me go away from home for a whole week. I was sure I had started to grow up.

The Fair

The state fair was held every summer in Jackson. Many from our school or church attended. A day would be designated, usually by the school principal, and the plans were announced at school so that everyone would have the same information regarding the day, the time, and where to meet up at the schoolhouse, as well as how much the bus ride would cost. It was a quarter each way. We always met at school because that was a convenient meeting place. When the day came, Cousin Glossie was up there waiting for everybody to board the big yellow school bus he had parked on the grounds. Every student who wanted to go had signed up ahead of time, and we piled on the bus for the almost two-hour ride to the fairgrounds. We sang songs along the way, like "Row, Row, Row Your Boat."

Every one of us had looked forward to the state fair. We got there at about eleven in the morning, and the sun was starting to get hot. Cousin Glossie told us what time to be back at the bus, and then off we went. The fair had all the usual stuff: cotton candy, canned goods, pies, all kinds of preserves, and hand-crafted articles like boxes that all fit into one. We saw different tools of all kinds, farm stuff like shovels, hoes, hammers and some weird plows and saws. There were the usual attractions, such as half-naked girls behind a curtain on a stage (we were too young to go in and see them). There was a woman who was so fat that all she could do was sit in a chair and point to the extra layers of fat on her body, and there were a couple of midgets playing a game on a stage. They must have been a husband and wife team.

Many rides were for small children, and the Ferris wheel appeared to be for lovers, but anyone could ride it, of course. It was about 80 degrees and getting hotter, so off came the light sweaters, and short sleeves were all you could see. We walked around eating cotton candy, hot dogs, and ice cream cones stacked up at least three scoops high, and we drank soda pop while we enjoyed the sights and watching people who came from different parts of the state. It was an exciting outing. When it was time to leave, I was ready, because my feet were tired and my whole body just wanted to stretch out and rest. But we had that two-hour ride on the bus back home. Most of us just curled up the best way we could in our seats and tried to sleep. It was a quiet ride back for Cousin Glossie. I couldn't wait to get home and fall into bed.

Because it was summer and school was out, the earliest I'd see any of my friends again after the fair would be at church the next third Sunday or when we got a chance to visit each other. We talked about the fair, remembering how hot it was and all the ice cream we ate, the cotton candy, the hot dogs and, of course, the two midgets on the stage. We relived the whole fairground experience until the next time we went.

The Old Drunk

When I was fifteen years old, I was driving up the road to the store and was flagged by an old drunk. I knew who he was; he was related to Papa. Anyway, I stopped. He walked right over and propped his foot up on the fender, rattling change in his pocket. I knew immediately he was drunk, so I put the truck in gear and asked, "What do you want?"

"You want some money to buy some candy?" he asked.

"You go to hell," l said. "I'm going to tell Papa."

I floored the gas and he almost fell. Dust was flying and I was mad. I couldn't wait to get back down to the house to tell Papa. He was plowing in the back field, and after he heard my story, he said, "You go back up to the house and sit on the porch with your Mama." I did just that. Papa was right behind me. He put the mule and the plow in the barnyard and left in his pickup truck. Nothing like that ever happened again. I was not afraid.

My experience with the old drunk reminded me of the time when Mama and Papa got into a big, serious argument. I don't remember what it was about, but they did argue sometimes. Anyway, Papa made the mistake of raising his hand, I think, as if to hit Mama. We were already standing in the doorway listening and wondering what was going to happen. Myrtis ran and attacked Papa from the back, and Jimmy and I grabbed him by his legs and pulled him as hard as we could. He could not have hit Mama if he tried. Mama just stood right there; she didn't move one inch. "You better not hit me, Noah. Don't you hit me. I can run this farm with my boys. You can leave. I can run this farm." Mama wasn't scared.

After that experience, when I was about ten years old, I was never afraid of anybody. Thinking back when Boy Noah was living at home after the war, the one thing I liked about him (because I didn't like his drinking) was what he did when Mama and Papa argued. He would walk up the hall from his bedroom and stand in the doorway, complaining: "Can't nobody sleep with this noise — nobody can sleep!" and they stopped. I could then go back to sleep. I don't think Myrtis and Jimmy woke up, but I always did.

I would talk back or curse in a minute, to anybody. At our basketball games, or when we were at another church singing, if I saw any of the older men look like they were flirting with the young girls, I had something that I could tell Papa. I argued that some of them were no good. I would say exactly what I thought to them and tell Papa.

My First Crush

"Good girls don't." "It's wrong." "You must wait until you are grown." "Wait until you are married" "You must wait...."

Those were the only remarks Mama and Papa ever made about sex and marriage, and there were only been three kinds of occasions for those clear and simple statements. The first was the day I became a woman. The other two were in the face of rumors when either a girl got pregnant or there were "affairs" going on in the neighborhood. Mama used to sit and rock on the front porch with Carzella and carry on about Dan, Paul, Clifford, and Tootsie having so many pretty girl-friends. "They must really be something," Mama used to say. That "something," to my mind, had to be about sex, without Mama or Carzella ever saying it. Why were they talking like this? Was I simply to believe everything they were telling me, or was there more to it than protecting a young girl?

One day, a beautiful boy came to visit me from far away. He had lived near us in my childhood, but by the time he returned many years later, I hardly recognized him. It didn't matter. I was so struck by the boy standing on my doorstep that I was just relieved he was someone I already knew.

"C'mon in, Lenny. Well, you sure have filled out," Mama greeted him. "Have you been playing in a lot of sports over there in Alabama?"

"Yessum, Miss Exposé," Lenny answered politely.

He was from Birmingham, a big city bustling with culture and politics. He must be very sophisticated by now, I thought. What will he do here? "Ma'am," Lenny asked bashfully in his creamy voice, "could I ask your permission to take Charlene for a ride over to Fanny Mae's house to visit for a while?"

"That's fine — as long as you take Larry and Lynda over with you."

My little niece and nephew were about four and five years old, and just as ready to go riding as anyone could be. So into Lenny's pretty Buick we all piled — kids in the back and "grown-ups" in the front. Lenny drove the long way there, not up past the schoolhouse, but down old Rocky Branch Road, which went over to the crossroads store where we generally shopped for groceries. I was sitting in the front seat next to Lenny, looking out the window and riding by the old wooden bridge just down from Old Mr. Harris's house. The gravel road was as dusty as could be, but so many green trees lined the roadside with small, wooden houses tucked behind them, some painted and some not. The radio played. Could it possibly be? The radio was playing my song.

"For Your Precious Love" drove me wild inside every time I heard it, and now I was speechless. It said everything, or at least all either of us needed to hear.

I felt as if I were seeing everything for the first time. Children playing in the yards. Old men and women rocking in brown, wooden rocking chairs on the front porches. My head was peaceful. Everything was peaceful, quiet, floating in waves. Birds flew high in the open sky. Lenny was my first love. Occasionally, he held my hand and a warm feeling tingled through my whole body. I didn't know what he was thinking, but it didn't matter, because I was feeling a special closeness to him all on my own. I looked at him behind the wheel — his full chest and smooth, brown skin shown off by his classic white shirt, Levis, and brown oxfords. He had a head of soft, "good" hair that he let go natural. His smile was shy. We talked about school, Dan and Paul, how I liked basketball, and what I planned on doing with my life. Though he was a city boy, he was not at all intimidating, but kind and soft-spoken and his touch on my face was gentle.

To me, the boys in my school were all friends. They were boys I grew up with, went to church with, and whose parents knew Mama and Papa. I never saw them as anything else, no matter how they saw me. I'm sure one or two of them had eyes for me, but that was okay because I had a sweetheart who lived far away and I could always dream.

Paul was discharged in 1955 and we couldn't have been happier. We had our "going anywhere, anytime" life back. Studying brick masonry in Prentiss, Mississippi, and what he had already learned from Papa, Paul had become real good. We were older and could drive the car and go many places by ourselves. With Paul, it was perfect.

In school, we were writing school plays and performing them, having spelling contests, decorating the chapel for events. On Friday afternoons, Professor Price showed movies. We watched Roy Rogers and Dale Evans with Trigger. Hop-A-Long Cassidy, Lash La Rue with the whip, Fuzzy, Q. Jones and Wild Bill. A continuation series with Eddie Rochester that left us hanging on our seats in suspense, waiting for the next series.

There was a white traveling preacher who preached on the courthouse square in downtown Columbia on Saturday afternoons. This same preacher came to our school and taught us Bible verses in the early morning, starting with the first letter in the alphabet and going A through Z. We all had to learn the verses and stand up before the whole group of students and recite one memorized verse he taught us. I don't know how he came about coming to our school. He was different and white.

Anytime we had an auditorium full of people, and at the end of the gathering, the "Negro National Anthem" was sung: "Lift Every Voice and Sing." It was the norm for us. The other big gym was in the colored Columbia High School. We went there, as did everybody who could, to see Sam Cooke and the Soul Stirrers, the Five Blind Boys of Alabama, and the Reverend C.L. Franklin from Detroit, Michigan. Everybody came out to the auditorium for this night—church folks, parents and teachers alike, and students everywhere. It was packed full of folks. The old folks in the city of Columbia came. This event didn't happen often, so it was more than special for all of us colored folks. The fact that they were religious made it more of an event because everybody and anybody went to church, and having these famous people come all the way down to Mississippi to entertain us was indeed special. We got to see a little of what it must be like being in the big city with famous people you could see anytime. I think we saw the Staple Singers at Owens Chapel Church once in Columbia, Mississippi.

In 1957, Paul had a '57 Fairlane Ford, and of course he let me drive it. It was slicker than Papa's '55 Chevy. The Fairlane was a hot car — long, sleek, and pretty, and it could go fast. I used to cruise down Highway 24, going to town and thinking how good I looked. Sometimes, if there wasn't too much traffic on that isolated stretch of road leading to the downtown area, I would get that Fairlane up to seventy or eighty miles per hour and think how Papa would kill me if he knew I was driving so fast. As I got closer to town, I'd slow down to the speed limit, which was probably fifteen to twenty. This was fun for me, and I always wanted to drive that car, and maybe I would need that speed at some time.

Downtown Columbia on Owens Street was Albert Boothe's place. There was also a "juke joint" across the street, but Albert Boothe's place was where Paul and Dan would drop us off. They trusted him with us being in there. He also knew Papa. Jimmy, Dolly, and I would sit at a table and drink Cokes. The music would be playing on the juke box, and no sooner than we sat down, a boy came over and wanted to dance. If he looked OK—clean and dressed right and not talking any jive—we'd dance. Albert Boothe watched every move the boy made so he didn't hold us too close, or put his hand on my butt. We saw other schoolmates there also, and sat together. There was a room off the main entrance with a few steps down where the grown folks played cards and drank. We could not go in there, so we'd peep in the door. Every now and then, we'd see some man or woman from our community, and they'd try to hide their faces from us because we recognized them.

We danced to Ruth Brown's "Mama, He Treat Your Daughter Mean," Fats Domino's "Ain't That a Shame" and "Blueberry Hill," Little Richard's "Tutti Frutti," Clyde McPhatten's "The Great Pretender," Chuck Berry's "Johnny B. Good," and many others. We'd dance till my feet hurt and I was good and ready when Paul came by to pick us up. The juke joint across the street and one on the lower end of town, where all the other colored folks hung out, were not as popular as Albert Boothe's place. Coloreds lived down there. We never told Papa we were going there, and he never told us not to. We looked forward to dancing and seeing our friends there—a little different from school and church.

The Fight

I got into a fight when I was in the eleventh grade, and to this day, I feel that if you have to defend yourself, you must do so. I went all the way through elementary and secondary school without fighting, always managing to find my way out of it, either by talking or, if the other person had a weaker personality, just walking away. Sometimes I really wanted to fight because I felt the other person needed the crap beat out of them. They usually backed down, though.

That fight during my eleventh year of school was not of my own doings. One of my "friends" decided that she wanted to see some physical action. Obviously, because she thought she was my friend, she thought it was okay for her to post a nasty note on the bulletin board and sign my name to it. I knew who was responsible, but it was too late and too bad for me, because then I had to defend myself when the girl who was named in the note came right out of the blue and hit me. My response was to just hit her back, without even knowing why she hit me in the first place. After a few licks, she tried to stop long enough to tell me why she started the fight, but by that time, it was too late. Too many licks had been exchanged, and we were into a full-fledged fight. I won because Paul had taught me how to duck, punch, and block.

The principal, Mr. Dillon, called us into his office. Mr. Kelly, the math teacher, had already gotten to us, and he told me to just shut up and not say anything in the principal's office. For me, keeping quiet was worse than the fight. I couldn't stand not telling the principal what had happened, but somehow I managed. Mr. Dillon gave us a lecture about behavior, about how fighting looked to the younger students, about how we, as high school juniors, had to show better discipline, and how we had to be role models for the other students. I hated that lecture. It was unbearable sitting there, listening and not being able to defend myself, but I did it. Mr. Dillon put us both on two-day suspension, so we had to stay home for those two days.

Everything would have been all right, except at the supper table that night Darlene said, "I wonder who it is that can't go to school tomorrow?" No one said anything. A few minutes later, Jimmy said, "It sure ain't me." Finally, Papa asked, "Who is it that can't go to school tomorrow?" So I said, "I can't, Papa, 'cause I got into a fight and Mr. Dillon sent me and the other girl home for two days." I finally had it all out.

Papa asked, "Did you win the fight?" And I answered, "I sure did."

He kept right on eating. Mama said, "Now Charlene, you know better than to be fighting in school, or fighting at all."

"But Mama, she started it, and I couldn't just stand there and let her hit me," I said.

"Well, you know better," Mama said.

"Yessum, Mama," I said.

Paul's lessons of fighting came in handy one other day. The boys' basketball team was finished practicing and ran into the cafeteria, all sweaty, musty-smellin', and out of breath. They jumped into the middle of the line, pushing and shoving. One boy pushed me out of line as he was wiping his sweaty face. I balled up my fist and hit him right in the chest as hard as I could. His arms were up and that lick of mine was right on center. He hit the floor and the other players gathered around. One shook him and another poured water on his face. By that time Professor Steele had come in.

"What happened" he asked.

"He pushed me out of line," I said.

Professor Steele told the boy he would not tolerate players pushing anyone out of line. He didn't say a word to me about hitting him. We all went on in to eat. The blessing was done by different students, this day by Harvey. He clapped his hands to get our attention, and everybody got quiet. He mixed up the verses just to make it funnier. "The Lord is my Shepherd, so I don't want," or "In my Father's house is a penitentiary." The whole cafeteria was laughing and waiting for the next day.

The Prom

It was 1953 at the end of the school year and 1954 was coming. Myrtis would be graduating soon, and her junior and senior proms were the most important thing going on. The whole school would be excited. When the time came in April for Myrtis's junior prom, Jimmy, Darlene and I already knew what she was going to wear, who she was inviting, how she would act at the prom, which of her classmates she was going to sit at the same table with — just about everything. This was because that's all Myrtis talked about for two months.

Papa gave Mama the money to buy her dress and shoes. We went to downtown Columbia whenever we needed store-bought clothes. Mama could sew, but she didn't make us very many clothes. I think it was because she didn't sew especially well, even though she had three sisters who were practically tailors they were so skillful. This was no reflection on Mama — she just didn't put a lot of her energy into sewing. She limited it to household items. Our Sunday dresses, prom gowns, and some of our school clothes were store bought.

The day before the prom, my married sister, Carzella, who was a beautician and lived up the road, pressed and curled Myrtis's hair. Myrtis didn't like the curls to be too tight. She wanted them loose enough so that she could comb her hair out and make it look fuller, like it was relaxed, instead of tight curls.

There was always a group of boys and girls selected from each class as organizers. They consisted of juniors and seniors who were responsible for decorating the school chapel the afternoon before the prom. Myrtis was with the decorating group that year. I remember her putting a big scarf around her head to keep the dust out of her hair. When she returned home after decorating the chapel, Jimmy, Darlene, and I sat around the bedroom to watch her get dressed. Mama didn't wear lipstick or rouge, just a little powder on her face. I think her style influenced all of us because the whole makeup thing was never an issue. Even though girlfriends and teachers at school wore makeup, I never had any desire to wear it. Anyway, Papa wouldn't have let us go out of the house wearing a lot of lipstick. He'd say, "That's too much paint on your face." It seemed like only a little to us, but Papa would say, "You all look pretty enough without it."

The next year I watched Myrtis go through the same thing for that year's prom. At that time, I was in the ninth grade. My sister Jimmy was in the tenth grade at the time, but the next year she was in her junior year. Once again, the excitement of talking about dresses and boys was in the air. The closer I got to the time when I would go to my own proms, the more real they were becoming for me. When the time finally did come, the excitement of getting a pretty dress to wear and being all dressed up was different from getting dressed up to go to church. I knew I'd be out with my classmates, seeing what they were wearing and who they were with, and dancing 'til my feet hurt. I knew the teachers would be dressed up prettier than the rest, and that one of our male math teachers, who wore suits to school every day, would look better than the principal.

After Myrtis left for college in September 1954, we were on our own. It was me, Jimmy, and Darlene until Dan and Paul returned from the army. Again, school and church activities continued to fill our time. Playing basketball is what we did — just like playing the piano from Loretta on down. Jimmy and Pixie played some basketball. Darlene never got into it the way we did. We drove Papa's car sometimes and always the pickup truck — all riding in the same car, depending on who could drive.

It seemed like everything I'd done over the years, especially working the fields, wasn't that bad, I began to think about graduation and going away to nursing school. One Sunday, we went to church in the Lampton community, and a woman stood up as a guest and talked about her experiences as a registered nurse lieutenant in the army. She was born and raised in that community, so everybody knew who she was. This woman's name was Angie, and Papa and Mama knew her parents. She was very impressive in her uniform, and right then I knew

I wanted to be a nurse. At twelve years old, I never had to think about what I'd be when I grew up.

For my class at school to be ready for the prom, we had to start the preparations pretty early that year because we had plans for a small band, probably four or five musicians, to play for us. The band would have to include at least a piano player, who was usually the soloist, and also a drummer, and a guitarist if we were lucky.

My friend Bobbi was good at knowing how to raise money. We had set up a hot dog and hamburger stand at the Lampton gym during the ball games to raise money for the yearly social, and we also set up a stand to raise money for the prom. The good thing was that there was a small grocery store a couple of doors down from the gym where we could go to buy buns, hot dogs, and anything we needed when we ran out of supplies. In one area, we had someone assigned to the grill, and in another area two of us prepared the sandwiches after the meat was cooked. One person handled the soft drinks and the money, which was usually kept in a shoe box behind the counter. We never lost any money, and we never got ripped off.

A couple of times, I picked eight or ten crates of green beans or potatoes, loaded them on the back of Papa's pickup truck, took them downtown and sold them to the market. It paid off, because by the time the prom came around, I had enough money to buy my dress, and we had enough from our hot dog sale to pay each band member ten dollars for the night's work. The only other thing to do after raising the money was to decorate the chapel.

Carzella curled my hair the day before so it would look fuller and not so tight. By this time, Mama just handed me the money that Papa had given her to buy my dress. With that money, along with what I made boxing up potatoes and green beans and selling them to the market downtown, I was able to go downtown by myself to buy my dress. I chose an off-the-shoulder, white net dress with a scarf that was worn around the shoulder. A small row of multicolored plastic flowers decorated the waist. The dress was three-quarter length instead of full length, and I wore it with a pair of white satin, medium high-heeled shoes. The dress fit around the breast, and since I hadn't filled out quite that much yet, I had to tuck a sock into each side to help fill out that area.

The preacher's wife sold Avon products, so I already had some Avon cologne and face powder. That was just about it for the makeup department. My sister Darlene was three years younger, and she did what Jimmy and I had done years earlier — sat on the bed and watched while each of us got dressed for the prom. Jimmy and I both went to the prom my junior year because Jimmy was in the twelfth grade then. She was more relaxed about the prom because she had gone the year before. I gave her some of the money I had made from selling the potatoes and green beans to help buy her dress that year.

My date was a boy who was a friend of my brothers Dan and Paul. Mama had already told me that I was going to drive Papa's car up to the school myself and meet the boy there. Jimmy's date was a local friend Mama also agreed could meet up at the schoolhouse. I did the driving because I could drive better than Jimmy.

Once we finished dressing and came through the living room and into Mama's and Papa's room, Mama said, "You all look so pretty." Papa looked up over his specs. After spitting a mouthful of tobacco into the fireplace, he said, "You look just like your Mama." He told us to be back by midnight and we were. The car keys were always kept on the fireplace mantle, and I got them while Jimmy was looking at herself in the dresser mirror in Mama's room. Mama said, "Your dress is real pretty."

We walked slowly out the front door onto the porch, down the walkway to the car. It was warm and pleasant outside, so it felt good to have an off-the-shoulder dress. I knew there would be big fans in the schoolhouse chapel because they'd been put in place when we were there earlier helping with decorations and table arrangements.

When we got up there and parked, the boys were standing on the patio at the entrance of the chapel. Each of them had a small, white box with a white corsage in it. They took out the corsages, and I put mine on my wrist, because my dress had flowers at the waist. Jimmy's corsage went on the waist of her white dress. The boys were dressed up in black suits and bow ties. They looked good, yet behaved like just our good friends.

I sat at a table with one of my classmates, Bobbi, and her date, and Jimmy and her date sat with their classmates at another table. After we said hello to each other and sat down, the boys immediately got up and got us a cup of punch. While they were gone, Bobbi pulled out a tube of her lipstick from her small pocketbook and said, "Oh, just put on a little lipstick." I said, "I can only wear a little." "Yea," she said, "but all you have to do is wipe it off before you get home." We laughed and I put on some red lipstick, looking into a little powder container that had a small mirror in it. It was fun because I knew I wasn't supposed to wear that lipstick. Just then, the boys came back with the punch, and my date smiled as he noticed the change in my lips.

All my classmates were there and everybody was all dressed up and looking good, the girls in prom dresses and the boys in black suits. The band sang and played popular tunes, like Jerry Leiber and Mike Stoller's "Poison Ivy," and "Yakety Yak." The band played more fast numbers than slow ones. It seemed everybody who could dance well was out on the floor with every number, but with the slow tunes, the not-so-good dancers got up to dance as well. I was on the floor all the time, either with my date or with one or two of my friends I knew were good dancers. The prom marked the close of another year of school, along with the commencement exercise, which was the year's final activity. Usually, it was for somebody else, but this year it was for me.

I looked forward to graduating because that meant I would be going away to college somewhere. Mr. Dillon was my principal, and he always saw to it that every student got information and applications from various colleges and universities in the state of Mississippi and other states as well. He had a book we could use to look up the address of a particular school and write for an application. Before all of that, though, the prom came again at year's end and because I had attended two proms by now, the twelfth grade prom would be easy to prepare for. I knew exactly what I wanted — the color of my dress and shoes, and who I wanted to invite.

The other event of the twelfth grade was writing out my salutatorian speech for graduation. One of my friends was the valedictorian. She always earned a few more points than I did on exams, papers, quizzes, and the like, all the way through high school, but it was okay with me. I never felt inadequate about my abilities and Mama and Papa didn't drill me or any of my sisters and brothers to make us competitive. They just wanted each of us to do the best job we could.

My oldest sister, Loretta, had taught English in downtown Columbia at the colored high school years earlier, and the principal for that school gave my graduation speech. As salutatorian, I was acknowledged during the program along with the valedictorian and others in my class for distinctive achievements throughout the year. Mr. Dillon introduced us to the guest speaker after the program was over. During his speech, he talked about growing up and leaving home for the first time, about going to college, studying hard, and becoming a success. He talked about getting a job, taking care of yourself, and not being under your parents' wing anymore. He talked about how some before us had done the same things that were ahead of us now, how some had made it and others did not do so well. He explained how the opportunities were out there and we had to go after them. For me, these were the things Papa and Mama had said during my childhood. They never sat down and talked about these things specifically, but they showed me the best way to make them happen throughout my childhood, so most of this was very familiar to me.

The speaker talked about Booker T. Washington, Frederick Douglass, and men and women in our neighborhood who were respected and had done a lot for people. They were not all college-educated men and women. As I sat there, I thought more and more about Mama and Papa and how they had an eighth-grade education and both of them were smarter and wiser than I was. Their wisdom was in knowing what was best for me and my brothers and sisters, in disciplining us, teaching us right from wrong, how to be fair with people, not jumping to conclusions, and not talking about others. They expected me, along with my sisters and brothers, to go to college and get an education, but they were not dogmatic about it. It was something they instilled in me from a very early age, at about the time I started school.

I felt sad about leaving home and all my friends there. Thinking about them, sitting there, I felt a sadness mixed with excitement about graduating and going away to college. The realization that I'd be leaving Mama, Papa, and Darlene, the last three at home, was bittersweet. The guest speaker was talking and surely had no idea of what was going on in my head or the heads of the other students sitting there, but he continued and talked about faraway places—Paris, France, and Notre Dame. It was more than foreign to me because I had only been to Washington, D.C., and only a few places in the whole state of Mississippi, including Jackson, the capital, on the Gulf Coast, Biloxi and Gulfport. Paris, France, was across the water and that was a long way from home and from the United States. My ears perked up and I listened more carefully as he talked about how big the building of Notre Dame was and how when a voice up front at the podium spoke, it could be heard very clearly all the way in the back of the building. It was like a dream to me, of something I could not at that time see coming true. I felt that I would travel around the United States for sure, but I was not so sure of going across the water.

The commencement exercise left me with a lot of hope, energy, and a strong will to achieve — with confidence and the will to be persistent until I reached my own goals. Walking up to Mr. Dillon and getting my diploma was the end of an era, and of growing up, finally. The future was before me, the beginning of the next part of my life.

Chapter 7

The Family

In the countryside of Marion County in southern Mississippi, a small gravel path lies off an old blacktop road. The path leads to an old homestead with open pastures and fields. About an acre of land was cleared not too long ago next to a thick area of woods. Already it has some overgrowth of tall grass. I walked into the woods, pushing back long, prickly green vines and intertwined branches blocking my path. The ground was blanketed with brown leaves. I stooped under the limbs of trees and stepped over rotting logs. The trees were far enough apart for me to walk between them; most were upright despite the many wind and rain storms here in this part of Mississippi. The sun shone between the trees and there were no shadows because it was noontime.

About twenty feet into the woods, I came upon two headstones. The top halves had broken off and had been leaned against the bottom sections. These were the headstones of my great grandparents, Elias and Margaret Exposé. What remained of the upper part of Elias's headstone was split down the middle. Both headstones stood above footrests, except Margaret's footrest had shifted about twelve inches to the side. The writing on both headstones was easily read as the letters were constructed out of cement. Only the bottoms of the broken headstones that touched the ground were dirty.

IN MEMORY OF
E.L. EXPOSÉ
BORN AUGUST 29, 1838 DIED JUNE 10, 1891
ASLEEP IN JESUS

IN MEMORY OF MARGARET
WIFE OF ELIAS EXPOSÉ
BORN MAY 10, 1844 DIED SEPT 4, 1898
HONORED, BELOVED AND WEPT HERE MOTHER LIES

I stood and looked from one to the other, reading what was on them and shaking my head from side to side. It was like finally meeting someone I already knew. I had a feeling of calm inside and happiness.

My cousin had led me to the site. He had stumbled upon it by accident twenty years earlier while helping a neighbor fix a fence to contain some cows. He grew so excited, and a little scared, when he read the names that he quit work right then, went home as fast as he could, and told his grandma, my Aunt Sarah. She, along with Papa, my brother Tootsie, and other family members had known about the graveyard all along. The site was located within walking distance from Grandpa Daniel's old homestead and two miles from our house.

A few days after my visit to the graveyard, I met with the white owners of the farm, whose family had owned the land since the 1920s. They knew some colored people were buried there but did not know the circumstances of how they'd come to be there. In the past, they had cleaned around the site. Papa had told us the story of Elias, a runaway slave boy of fourteen years from northern Mississippi. He had marks on his back from beatings due to his many attempts to escape. Because he was out in the weather so much, the old slave master had given him the last name Expose. It is believed his real last name might have been Foxworth. Another slave boy, who would wash himself and "waller" around in a puddle of water, was given the last name Waller. During Elias's escapes, he became friendly with the swamps, traveling day and night and living off the land, surviving on blackberries, blueberries, nuts and the fruit of trees. He crossed paths with other runaways as well as freed colored folks who were working their farms and providing for their families. His spirit was never broken. He worked at any job he could, on farms picking cotton, cutting and hauling logs, construction, or working on farm equipment. A young, strong, and muscular boy, he learned to do many things on the farm. Elias met a girl named Margaret; they married around 1860 and had nine children. Their children would all grow up to be landowners, farmers, and preachers.

The children worked alongside their parents until they were old enough to marry — moving away for any other reason was not common back then. Once the older boys married and started having children, the next oldest ones did the same. Elias and Margaret were hardly ever left alone when they got old. A grandchild or two always stayed with them; with so many, family connections lasted all their lives, continuing year after year, without a break between generations.

I found on record a deed of trust from Elias to two different men for his crop of cotton, corn, peas, and potatoes. It was for money loaned to him by the men — January 31, 1872. During my search of the Mississippi land record, I learned that Elias's oldest son, Stephen, was listed as his heir.

Elias's Boys— The Brothers Exposé: Stephen, Harry, Daniel, Willis, Paul, Silas

Uncle Stephen and Harry became known for their business savvy. Being the oldest, they set an example for the rest of their brothers and sisters, buying land that created whole communities. Daniel and Willis did the same. They also found themselves involved in physical confrontations right in the churchyard. Being a preacher did not hinder Willis in fighting. It took years for the youngest boys, Paul and Silas, to follow in their older brothers' footsteps, much less those of their father, Elias. In a roundabout way, they let go of their wandering ways.

The Voice: Stephen

Stephen, the firstborn of Elias and Margaret, had a voice that cleared your head, lifted your soul, and stole your heart. I don't know how he did it, but as he grew older, he used his voice as an organ of the church. Why, people could hear him from miles away. As they stood in his presence, which was as big-boned and burley as his songs were boisterous, they saw he cupped his hand over his ear and cut loose, as loud as he could, hitting every note, high and low. "Abide with Me," he often sang, or "Have Thine Own Way," and the walls of the church almost came tumbling down. Many churches throughout the countryside, Methodist and Baptist, invited Stephen to sing. He always went and felt honored to do so.

Great-uncle Stephen was a frequent participant in the devotional service; it was his domain. Farming as his father did, he lived in the Blue Spring community. Stephen and his wife had twelve children. Buying land whenever he could, he taught all his children the importance of land ownership and the independence it gave a Negro man. Hard work, education, and religion were their only ways of life.

The Postman General: Harry

Harry, the second-born son (in 1861) to Elias and Margaret Exposé, would grow up to become the postmaster general of Exposé, Mississippi. He was married and lived in the Improve, Mississippi, community for two years. Other family members lived nearby. Harry and his wife had five children and moved to a small community north of Columbia, Mississippi. Harry would buy and sell land all his life, most of which he homesteaded. His wife was heir to some swamp and woodlands called Old Pine Island. Farming was Harry's main livelihood, often from pulling the plow himself because the luxury of horses and mules was not for the Negro man at that time. Harry's education reached only to the second grade, but he learned to read and write and became a realtor and general store manager.

The first account of how Exposé was named was around 1905–1907. A petition was sent to Washington, D.C., for the Town of Exposé. It's believed that Governor Willoughby approved the petition. In 1907, the land was surveyed for Harry Exposé. It had six streets: First, Second, Third, Fourth, Main, and Center. The second account came from court records of a railroad company called the New Orleans Great Northern Railroad (later the Gulf Mobile and Ohio) that needed a strip of land on which to lay its tracks. The land was owned by Harry Exposé, and he was totally against it. As an incentive, the railroad company offered to name the town after him if he would sell the land for the track. Harry sold on that condition, according to the Marion County court records.

After the railroad track was built, the only means of transportation for the mail was the railroad. A depot was built and for a while the train would stop if it was flagged down or it had to drop off merchandise. When the mail went out, it hung on the "mail grab." The train slowed down just enough to grab the mail. The little depot post office was what brought Harry his claim to fame.

The train's main stops were Mendenhall, Columbia, and Lumberton. Under a small, unpainted wood frame that sheltered people from the rain and the sun, the depot provided a meeting spot for families and friends. The rhythm of the train could be heard for miles in the quiet countryside. "Chug-a-chug-a-chug-a-chug-a, tic-tic-tic, chug-a-chug-a," pounded the machine through the fields. Small cars sped alongside as horses galloped in fright. Children on the way to school ran away from the tracks. When it slowed, a whistle of steam poured out on the crowd that gathered from the surrounding fields. Dogs barked, pigs squealed, babies cried, hats shot up in the air. The train had arrived; each time, it felt like the Fourth of July.

At a cost of just twenty-five cents, farmers could travel by train from nearby Columbia to Prentiss, Mississippi, in no time at all. Women and children used the train to visit relatives on Sunday. Young people took it for joy rides just to get away for the fun of it. Harry, who was old and sickly by then, rode the train for medical and business reasons. A relative recalled seeing as a child riding to Jackson Negroes and whites sitting on opposite sides of the railcar. With more people coming into the community, a church was built, also a cemetery and a school that existed through the mid–1950s.

Harry's offspring still live in the Exposé community, up Highway 13 north of Columbia. The roadside is scattered with houses, most belonging to Harry's descendants. The St. John's National Baptist church in the Exposé community was torn down in 2006, which meant an important piece of Exposé history was being destroyed.

Grandpa Daniel

Grandpa Daniel was the fourth child and third son of Elias and Margaret Exposé, born March 12, 1868. He died June 6, 1945. Grandpa forged a living out of the land as his father and his two older brothers had done. Hard-working as he was, he found when he grew old enough to marry his new bride could work even harder. There was something about her coming from a half-white father that caused Grandma Eran to have a very strong work ethic, especially she being a girl. Grandpa bought land in an area straight back behind our house, where it stood. There, he and Grandma Eran raised two boys, Uncle Luther and Papa.

The old house was characteristic of the style of most houses of the time: a high-beam ceiling, a long central hall that went from the front door to the back, and a wide porch across the front. Grandpa and Grandma lived in that house from the time they were married until 1918. Papa and Uncle Luther worked the farm as young boys right alongside Grandma Eran and Grandpa. The only problem was that the soil was the worst ever, full of Bermuda grass and hard clay in many areas. Nothing grew well. Grandma's hands were calloused, almost bleeding, from digging and scraping that soil. Grandma just got tired.

Grandpa heard about a small farm up the road from our house that some old white man had for sale. Grandpa contacted him and made the deal to buy the farm. Grandma was satisfied. Now she not only had a pretty white house but also one with better soil. She could grow a better garden and strawberries. The old house was rented out by Grandpa, and later years by Papa, to a family that continued to farm the land for many years. My brother Tootsie said he, Boy Noah, and Clifford remembered the family that rented the old house and farmed on Grandpa's land. As a little girl, I remember the old, empty shell of a house and looking out the broken windows at what once had been cotton and corn fields.

The Preacher: Uncle Willis

The fourth son and sixth child of Elias would grow up to be a Methodist preacher. Married to Mathilda, one of Grandma Eran's sisters, Uncle Willis lived at Rosehill, another adjoining community. On Sunday, Uncle Willis was in the pulpit preaching; during the week, he was behind the plow in the fields, just like all the other men. Farming and buying land like his brothers before him is what he did. All seven of his children were raised in the tradition of farming the land.

On Sunday after church, I remember the indoor gatherings at Uncle Willis's house. A big table with a lot of chairs, some from the yard, filled the big open hallway off the kitchen. Children were everywhere — laughing, piano playing, and singing. The food was like at a picnic, but indoors. Fried catfish, green beans, rice, and soda pop were everywhere. Our relatives were on the front porch, in the yard, and throughout the house. Aunt Mathilda cooked for us all. It seemed like a celebration to me, but it was just a visit or get-together of the relatives.

The Dapper Brother: Uncle Paul

The fifth son and seventh child of Elias and Margaret was a real character. He's the special topic of uncles in the first chapter who's talked about by Papa and Thad Lampton. As Uncle Paul had been hosted by many of his brothers and various nephews in their homes, it was a shock when he finally settled down and became a land owner. Married twice, with children by both wives, a daughter from the second marriage is alive and living today in the Silver Cheek community above the Exposé community. All the older relatives had died, so it was my pleasure to meet her last year. Nell, Uncle Paul's daughter, whose beauty rivals any Broadway star of any age, smiled as she talked about her father and his flamboyant ways.

Uncle Cotton, or Uncle Silas

The sixth son and ninth child of Elias and Margaret was also a farmer. Uncle Silas was married to Pinkie, but they didn't have any children. He, too, spent many nights at relatives' homes — nephews, cousins, aunts, and uncles. As a child I remember him. He'd just show up in the front yard one day, carrying a little burlap sack thrown over his shoulder. He was tall and thin, with snow white hair, hence the nickname "Uncle Cotton." He was relaxed, with an easy way about him, very much like my brother Bufford.

Elias' Girls — The Sisters Exposé: Ocia, Mary, Emma

The glue that held the sisters together more than blood was the church. I never saw sisters that were more religious. The "Amens," "Thank you, Lords," and "Holy Fathers," were like echoes through the church. The rest of the congregation made their usual response to the scripture, the singing, and the sermon, but the sisters' responses were very distinct and lasted throughout the service.

During the revivals at Uncle Willis's church, all the family members would gather and drive down to his house. They spent the whole weekend; it was like a vacation for them all. The adults hunted and fished, and the children camped out during the night. In the afternoon, they all played games while the big picnics were getting going—cooking the fish and celebrating with family.

There were so many family members they practically filled the church, and Uncle Willis was in his glory. Of course, Aunt Mathilda and Grandma Eran would march Grandpa Daniel and Uncle Willis right out if they got out of hand, which they did sometimes, talking about their encounters at church.

Great-Aunt Ocia

The first girl of Elias and Margaret was small in stature, but strong when it came to hard work. Ocia and her husband had five children and they lived in the Bassfield community. Farming they did, and taught their children hard work and the value of education. Religion was the norm. Their children became musicians and teachers. A grandson, Philip, sang in a quartet with one of the Lee boys, the Magee boys, and others. Many nights Philip stayed down at our house after singing away from home. He'd spend the night and catch the bus the next day from our school, LaMarion, to return home. He served in World War II in 1942 and the reserves for many years until he retired from active duty in 1985. He became the band director at Higgins High School where he wrote the school anthem, which is still played today. In Clarksdale, Mississippi, they all remember him. He moved back home to Bassfield and lived there until his death in January 2012. I felt fortunate to have met him before he died.

Great-Aunt Mary

There's not much I remember about Aunt Mary except her shouting and praising the Lord in church with her sisters. The information given on the 1910 census indicates she had seven children—four boys and three girls. Living in the Blue Spring community, she was close to all her brothers and sisters.

The African Queen: Great-Aunt Emma

Aunt Emma, the eighth child, would grow up to be flamboyant. "Praise the Lord"—you could see her coming by the big head wrap, elaborate and colorful. Tall, large, and dark, she strutted her grandiosity, so to speak, in more ways than one. She looked like an African woman in the lovely concoctions she wore. The multiple layers of flowing skirts, topped by long, fancy aprons and brilliant shawls and scarves, were outnumbered only by the beads around her neck and the bracelets on her ample arms.

Aunt Emma would parade into church as if she were a sedan of clouds in a sunrise sky. As Uncle Willis preached, she hummed a private hum, publicly announced. "Yes, Lord ... Yes, dear Lord." She built up a rhythm: "My Jesus ... Yes, Lord ... My Jesus ... Help me, Lord." And then before you knew it, she was up in the aisle, walking, talking, moaning, sighing, sobbing, possessed by the Lord. Eyes rolled, jaws dropped, people swayed, and Aunt Emma undulated in her own personal heaven of praise and forgiveness, comfort, and joy. Aunt Emma was all the entertainment we needed when we went to church. She was the high point of the whole service.

As the eighth child of Elias and Margaret, she was next to the youngest, and she lived to be one hundred and three. Married to Uncle Andrew Magee, she had five children, who followed family tradition and farmed the land. Religion, education, and treating people right was their way of life.

Uncle Luther: Papa's Brother

Visiting Uncle Luther and Aunt Pearlie was as homey as we could get. Uncle Luther, two years older than Papa, was born in 1891. He was a good match with Grandpa Daniel in telling stories and tall tales. He kept us wide-eyed and open-eared for long periods, spinning yarns. Aunt Pearlie would calmly walk back and forth between the stove and the table top and sink, stirring butter beans and mixing cornmeal for corn bread. She was as wide as she was tall and always smiling and humming, her big hips swaying back and forth.

Uncle Luther would be busy chewing tobacco and spitting in his little can beside his chair as he watched her every move, telling me, Jimmy, and Myrtis how he courted Aunt Pearlie. He didn't get married until he was thirty-seven years old. Although he and Aunt Pearlie had no children, he certainly claimed to have had them by other women. There were two, a boy and a girl, that he acknowledged.

Uncle Luther was a dapper dresser and sometimes carried a cane, just like Grandpa Daniel. He farmed, but on a much smaller scale than Papa, and he did very little carpentry work. The one thing he did routinely, with Mr. Ado Lee, was to walk up to the Improve store to catch a ride to downtown Columbia. They sat around on the courthouse square chewing tobacco; smoking, talking about everything, and watching the people go by, especially the women. This routine never failed.

As young boys, Tootsie said Uncle Luther would take them along on some of his dates with the pretty girls he was courting, especially when he drove them home from church or some other social gathering. The tales were sometimes about girlfriends he may or may not have had, but the tales sounded good.

Uncle Byron

Sitting on the edge of Aunt Sarah and Uncle Byron's porch, the way we did at Grandma's or Uncle Luther's, was all the same. I didn't know any difference. Uncle Byron was Uncle Byron, and Aunt Sarah was the same as Aunt Pearlie. Farming was their life and religion was as well.

Great Grandpa: Hardi Lee

Grandma Eran's father was married twice and had children by both marriages. On the census, he's labeled as a "mulatto" for race. Grandma, who was very fair-skinned, had various sisters and brothers, both fair-skinned and dark. Grandpa Daniel was dark-skinned, but he also had brothers that were fair-skinned.

Hardi Lee, Grandma Eran's father, sometime in the 1930s.

At Grandma's House

There were a few houses scattered about the countryside that were very similar. They were big and square with a high-pitched roof and columns across the front porch. A wide, open hallway went from the front door to the back door, all painted white with a gray shingle roof.

Mr. Ado Lee's house up the road was very similar, and another house in the community was also. I thought only white folks lived in houses like that, but Grandma and Grandpa did, as well as other colored families we knew. Grandma's house had six rooms. When you came from the front porch into the hallway, there were three bedrooms on the right side, and on the left were the living room, dining room, and kitchen. The living room had a couch and two chairs, a coffee table, and two end tables. Very hard, starched doilies that stood up around the lamps were on every end table. One doily just sat alone on the coffee table. All the tables were made of wood. The dining room had a big, wooden table with six chairs and a tablecloth that Grandma had made with a hand-knitted border. I'm sure it was made from bleached white flour sacks, just as the sheets and pillowcases were.

The kitchen had a big black iron stove and a couple of small tables Grandpa had built against the walls. A real old cabinet, unpainted, stored food and dishes. The three bedrooms had a fireplace between the two larger ones, and the third, smaller one behind Grandma's room was where we slept when we spent the night. A dresser with a big center round mirror and a low middle section sat in both rooms, also a wardrobe and chest of drawers. The small bedroom had a smaller chest of drawers. The mattresses were soft; you sank into them after climbing up on a step stool to get to them. The beds had wood frames and all the floors were made of wood. On the left side of the wraparound porch that went across the front was a cistern for storing rainwater; on the right side was grandma's strawberry patch.

Our visits to Grandma's were filled with adventure. Grandma would put on her garb — a big, straw hat, a long dress always, long sleeves, gloves, and lace-up shoes. She gathered up her buckets, one for her head and one for each hand. We got one small bucket. Down through the woods we went, way back to where there was a clear-morning spring of pure water. The path along the way was uneven and hilly, with rocks and dirt and all kinds of trees and vines. The bright sun shone through between the limbs. The birds made the only sounds. Grandma said the spring water had some kind of healing power, but she used it for cooking and to drink. It did taste fresh.

Strawberry-picking time was the best; we only got a small bucket or basket full each, but that seemed like a lot to us. I didn't know of anyone else who had strawberries. One summer, two of Grandma's sisters came to visit. One's name was Angeline. These sisters wore summer print dresses and strap shoes with the toes out, and they wore lipstick and long, black wigs. Jimmy and I took turns trying on one of the wigs in front of the dresser mirror in the bedroom. They dressed different from Grandma, but they looked like her. They showed us pictures of trees big enough to drive a car through. One sister was fair-skinned and one was dark. They laughed and talked a lot with Grandma.

Many days Grandma would walk down to our house with her basket of strawberries covered in a white, embroidery-edged towel. Way up the road to the hill, we could see her. There was nothing between her and our house then but fields and flat areas. The closer she got to the house, the more excited Jimmy and I became. We knew what the treats were. As she walked through the only dense, woodsy area before the clearing at the edge of the field across the road and the yard, Jimmy and I would set out running to meet her. She'd stop, open her arms wide and we'd just fall in. A big, wet kiss followed; what a relief. As soon as she turned her head, her spit was wiped off our faces with the tail end of our dresses.

Holding her hand, we carried the basket of strawberries to the house. Grandma and Mama would sit on the front porch and talk for a long time. Sometimes, Grandma walked back home, and other times Paul drove her back. We loved her visits because she didn't like Mama to whip us, and we knew it. We'd heard her say to Mama, "Mae, don't whip the children too much." That made us feel real good and maybe we could do a few more things around the house and get away with it. We were always figuring out a way not to get a whipping.

173

Grandma Eran and Grandpa Daniel Exposé in the 1920s.

Grandpa Daniel's Tall Tales

In the first long tale, Grandpa said he was walking down the road with only his cane, minding his own business. The other day at dusk, a big old black bear jumped out into the road right in front of him. He stopped, raised his cane, and told that old bear to git going 'cause he'd hit him. Right then, he saw a big rock on the side of the road. He picked it up as fast as he could and hit that bear right in the head. The bear stumbled, turned around, and wobbled back in the woods. Grandpa hightailed out, running as fast as he could, until he got back home.

"Grandpa, do we have bears down at the house?"

He said, "I don't think y'all have any, just me and your grandma."

174

One day, Grandpa said he saw Old Man So-n-So walking down the road, a man who had already died, and we laughed and laughed. The best visit was one day when Jimmy, Myrtis, Darlene and I were sitting on the front porch at Grandpa's. Except this was no tale. This time, it was true. We were eating tea cakes and drinking milk when we saw a pickup truck full of fat, little, dirty children in the back, and fat grown-ups in the cab of the truck. It came to a stop. Grandpa sat upright, and he put on that who-the-hell-are-you face. The fat woman stayed in the truck and all the little dusty-faced children lined up along the side of the truck looking at us, and we were looking at them. The fat man got out, walked through the gate, and came right up to the front porch. Grandpa stood up. "What do you want?" Grandpa asked.

"It sure is a nice day," said the man.

"Nice day, my foot. What do you want?"

"My name is John, and I'm here to show you how you can make some money."

"You can show me nothing, and you better get away from here, 'cause I know your name ain't John."

"But I can make you money. Now, if you go in and bring out a few dollars, I'll show you."

"Okay, Wait a minute," Grandpa said.

We just sat there, looking at the fat man. His fat wife came walking up the walkway and stood right there behind him. There was a bad smell when she came close. A few minutes later, Grandpa came back out onto the front porch. He had his shotgun in his hands, held it up, leveled it right over the man's shoulder, and pulled the trigger. "Now you git."

We never saw a funnier sight: two fat people running, dirty children screaming, and fat butts moving in every direction. That gun scared the hell out of them, and we laughed until I fell over. Jimmy and Myrtis were lying back on the porch floor, too, laughing.

In the wintertime, Grandpa would promise us red, juicy watermelons. We waited and waited and they never came. If we had to go in the kitchen, we went in pairs. It was too scary because there had to be some kind of boogie-man behind the door. Grandpa always told us to watch out for him

Grandpa let us do things we could not do at home, and say things we didn't dare say in front of Mama and Papa. After we had spent the night, Grandpa would wake us up real early so we could drink coffee with him at the dining room table. Jimmy, Myrtis and I would get our cups and saucers and sit down. His cup was bigger. The coffee pot was an old metal gray one, big enough for all of our cups. His prayer before we started drinking was two words, and the one he said before we ate food: "Jesus wept."

The steaming, hot, black coffee smelled up the whole house. He'd pour the coffee in all the cups, and we'd wait until Grandpa took his first slurp — slow and careful — then we followed. He'd pour a little in the saucer and slurp it. We did the same. No cream or sugar. He told us to drink it black so we could be black like him. After all, coffee made you black, he told us. Every now and then, he let out a curse word, and Grandma heard him. From the kitchen we'd hear, "Now Daniel, you be careful in there." She didn't want him cursing in front of us, but we loved it. We'd laugh and imitate him. We had no idea what he was saying.

Mama's Family: The Dukes

Anderson Dukes, Mama's paternal grandfather, was born a long time ago, in 1820. He and his wife, Viney, lived in Brookhaven, Mississippi. An old photograph shows Viney and daughter Mary standing on the front porch. There is no evidence that he was in the Civil War or any other war. He and Viney had seven children, according to the 1870 U.S. census. Anderson Dukes may have been Choctaw Indian because his sons and daughters were believed to be, or at least partially.

Their skin was yellow to fair, with hair straight or wavy. They had sharp facial features and thin noses and lips. Anderson was a farmer and there is no evidence he was ever a slave.

A cousin, Louise Hendricks Noel of Richmond, California, remembers that great grandpa Anderson and Viney lived in a very large family home in Brookhaven. The Dukes would become ministers, mechanics, doctors, artists, musicians, singers, avid fisherman, sharp-shooters and community leaders. Julia and Allen are the oldest of Anderson and Viney Dukes' children, and there is little to no information about them. Julia, 17, and Allen, 13 years old in 1870, were farmhands at home. The other children, ages two through eleven, were at home as well.

Grandpa Emanuel and Grandma Sophronia

"Uncle Man," as he was called, was the third child and second son of Anderson and Viney Dukes. He would also grow up to be a humanitarian in the community. An old black and white photograph of the church Emanuel founded hung in their house. The Baylis community just east of Columbia, Mississippi, was their home.

As a farmer and land-owner, Uncle Man owned many acres and grew cotton and corn and raised hogs, and chickens. Many vegetables were grown for his family, as well as fruit

Grandpa Emanuel Dukes, Mama's father, in the 1920s.

177

trees that he shared with his neighbors. Cousin Geraldine ("Little Bit") remembers rugs on the floor that looked like the material baskets were made from. Their high-post beds contained lots of mattresses, and the last one on top was full of feathers. Grandpa made the chairs and rockers from wood, with cowhide seats.

He was soft-spoken, kind, quick-witted and never too busy to answer all the questions his many grandchildren asked. He enjoyed fishing and hunting and called Grandma Sophronia "Mud." He allowed his daughters to hunt with their brothers and drive the A-model Ford. Little Bit remembers Grandpa preaching at his brother's church, Friendship Baptist, and how he would sing "There Is a Fountain" with tears running down his cheeks. Sitting in the pew up front, Little Bit wondered why he was crying. Did being a preacher-man mean you had to be strong? Or was it because he was going blind? Grandpa gave up the ministry in 1927, as he could see only shadows.

After a visit down to Grandpa's, Little Bit and her brother came home and found their mom and dad talking in very low voices. Aunt Sang had a long talk with her children, telling them to be good, love and stay close to all their sisters and brothers, get an education, and respect others. They were a little confused at that time with all the serious talk. They found out why very soon afterwards. A message was delivered that Grandpa had died. There were no telephones. It was 1936, and a very sad day for all. The casket was in the living room. Little Bit and her brother kept asking why Grandpa wasn't moving or breathing. They were told he was asleep and resting. They went up and brushed his hair and were not afraid. He was their Grandpa. I wish I had known him.

A former pastor of Columbia Valley United Methodist, the Reverend Ludrick Cameron, spoke along with many of the pioneers of Grandpa Dukes' church. They viewed a large collection of photographs my cousin Little Bit had. They spoke about Grandpa's vision and leadership qualities, how he encouraged the young to get an education no matter what field they chose, to use common sense, to be respectable,

and to have high moral stan-
dards. Grandpa was really
something as a man, husband,
father, brother, and friend. He
was pastor of a church in
Brandon Bay near Tylertown,
and a church in the Hub community. It was at that church
where he met his future bride,
Sophronia.

Grandma Sophronia was
the strong, hard-working
woman who supported her
preacher husband — raising the
children, working in the fields
with him, and maintaining the
household. Religion, education, and treating people right
was her way, and she enjoyed
embroidery, crocheting, and
quilting. Most of the discipline
was left up to Grandpa Emanuel, even though Grandma

Grandma Sophronia and Grandpa Emanuel in the 1930s.

could take over any of those duties. In my brothers' back bedroom,
there hung a tin picture of Grandma's pa, Gustave Jefferson. For years
it was a mystery because it was so old; it looked spooky.

Aunt Polly's Cookout: Grandma's Sister

She sat in her high-back chair and held court. It was one of the
many cookouts on her farm. Sister's grandchildren came from far and
wide — Harmony, First Hopewell, Exposé, and a few visiting from the
city. Cousin Geraldine and my brother Tootsie remember how they

179

traveled by horse and buggy down to Aunt Polly's home in Hub, Mississippi. She told stories of how she would talk to the old, white businessmen in Columbia, Mississippi, about their "stores," buying land, which Aunt Polly did, and about their families. Encouraging the young ones at her cookouts to try to own something when they grew up, land was the best, she told them, because owning it was life long. It wasn't hard for the children to listen because Aunt Polly's flamboyant, expressive behavior and good looks could hold the attention of anyone.

Washtubs of soda pop, big pots of collard greens, pans of cornbread, sliced tomatoes and cucumbers, fried fish, pans of potato salad, and watermelon — they ate it all. My brother and cousins looked forward to the next year's cookout.

Great-Uncle Gabriel: A Minister Also

Gabe Dukes was the pastor of Friendship Baptist Church, located a few blocks from Grandpa and Grandma's home. Sometimes Grandpa Dukes would preach with the Exposé family preachers, and the Dukes would all turn out to the church in support. It became a ritual that was enjoyed by all. Uncle Gabe's grandson, Lonnie, lived in Columbia, Mississippi, and he visited us on a regular basis. He was a lot of fun. Three of his sisters lived in Los Angeles, and I met them all, especially Burnell.

Uncle Gilbert: The Doctor

Uncle Gilbert would grow up to become a medical doctor in Dermott, Arkansas. He was a physician and surgeon specialist in diseases of women and children, and he was a 32nd degree Mason. During the summer months, Papa and Uncle Luther would go to Arkansas to work in the sawmills. They lived with Uncle Gilbert while they were there. Aunt Sang, his niece, was influenced by him to attend pharmacy school as a young lady.

Mary

Mary was Louise Hendricks Noel's grandmother. Cousin Louise lived in Richmond, California, and had great stories to tell about the Dukes. Her grandmother Mary worked for the Hugh White family, who lived in Columbia, Mississippi. As young children, Aunt Stella, Mary's sister, and Hugh White played together. Hugh would become governor of Mississippi and live in a mansion. When asked if she ever visited the mansion she said, no, she felt Hugh had forgotten about those days. Cousin Louise looked white, but let you know verbally that she was black.

Gilbert Dukes, Emanuel's brother, in the early 1900s.

Aunt Stella

I remember her as one of the fairest-skinned relatives of all. She came up from New Orleans to visit us on occasion. Mama would call us in — me, Jimmy, and Myrtis—from the field, barnyard, or wherever we were so we could come see her and speak to her. She always kissed us on the cheek. As soon as we left her and Mama, we would wipe off the kiss because we thought she was an old, white woman, and we laughed and laughed. The youngest of Anderson Dukes' children was John, and I have no information on him other than that he was two years old in 1870.

Grandpa Emanuel's Children

The Pretty Dukes Girls

SANG: CHICKEN WOMAN

Julia's sisters shared the same vision. To see that vision manifested, one need only to peep into their merriment decades later as they took stock of all they shared on a balmy spring night in 1938. Sarah Dukes, the eldest daughter in a family of nine, was as busy as a one-armed paperhanger. Cranking the hand-pump water faucet in her sink, she raced from one end to the other of the wall-to-wall, built-in cupboards in the kitchen of her finely crafted home near First Hopewell Baptist Church. Fresh-cracked golden meal found its way from her mill into the big baker's bowl that would hold the batter for that night's corn-bread. She dipped a tin cup into the barrel of flour standing on the pastry floor and tossed it into another bowl with salt and pepper. Soon enough, sputtering in a big, black pot on the stove was the freshest fried chicken for miles around.

Sarah (better known as "Sang") raised the chickens herself up to two-and-a-half pounds, at which point they were ready to sell at the market. Her incubator, hatching house, and brooding house were all constructed so that at any stage of their growth, the chicken would not be touching the ground. The profits from this thrifty enterprise might have looked like pin money to someone else, but in fact, she used them to send her oldest daughter, Thelma, to beauty school and then to Alcorn A & M College. Sang herself was a science wiz, and had been allowed to attend pharmacy school while living with her uncle, Gilbert Dukes, in Arkansas. She then became an insurance agent for Cook Galloway Funeral Home, where she guided the bereaved through their choice of caskets, burial plots, and tombstones.

Later, her domestic skills claimed her time. A master of needlework from embroidery to quilting, she also crocheted her own bedspreads

Grandpa Emanuel's family photograph from the early 1900s.

and tablecloths. Her white and multicolored doilies graced the backs of the chairs, chests of drawers, and fireplace mantles of her spotless house. A sharpshooter (taught by her brother Gilbert) and an avid fisherwoman, she also became an active member of the PTA, the Watts School, the 4-H Club, the Busy Bee Club, the Golden Links Tabernacle Hall, and the Eastern Stars. If it was there to do, she did it.

Everyone knew Sang for this reason. Let us not dwell on the dainty apron that sat pristine and pretty on Sang's tailored suit that she had cut and sewed from the finest wool. Lace-up boots covered her tiny feet, size 5A. With her high cheekbones and tresses falling softly along both sides of her well-sculpted face, there was music in her eyes. Sang had poured herself a glass of her own homemade wine.

183

Our visits to her were very exciting, interesting, and downright educational. With her milling, chicks, and wine-making, we learned a lot. To see how she worked around the house, and all the things she could do made me think women could do anything, even if they were pretty. And she was so smart. She taught her daughters to do embroidery, crocheting, and quilting.

Maude: The Little Woodchopper

Next to Sang stood her sister, Maude, who never could bake a cake — or a pie, for that matter — but she just came right out and took responsibility for her handicap by hiring two women from the Hub community to do the baking for her when it came time to take something to the annual revivals. Maude's deep-set eyes over her hollowed-out cheeks jeered at you while her square jaws just let out a wide grin, like she was much the wiser for it. She scurried around in "granny-style" dresses or a short smock over a long skirt and shirt for working in the fields; and she pulled them off along with her old boots to take a bath in the big washtub to change into a clean pink or blue dress for inside the house. Maude did a good bit of her own crocheting, showing off her popcorn stitch with such success that she had a thriving local market for it among the whites in Columbia and nearby communities, to whom she also sold quilts and embroidered linens as colorfully as her flower garden.

On a daily basis, Maude was working hard in the fields when she wasn't out as an insurance agent or at Washington Funeral Home, where she worked for twenty-five years. But on Sundays, she was at one with her chickens, ducks, little biddies, and fat turkeys who stretched their rainbow feathers as they gobbled to each other. She hitched up her own horse and buggy to get to her tabernacle meetings; and on those occasions, daughters Alice and Daisy, two of her nine children, and her husband, Joe Geeston, would be packed off to spend the night at Grandpa Emanuel's house.

Emanuel Dukes' house had a wraparound porch with a highly

cherished screened-in enclosure that added miles to the girls' reputations for bravery. There, they could boast that they had "slept outside" and be proud of their feat as "big" girls. Their dreams were still pint-size, because the minute Grandma Sophronia came to take the kerosene lamp back inside the house, up came the covers, hiding and protecting every goose bump of little-girl flesh from the boogie-man until time wore so heavily on them that their squirming bodies gave way to slumber even in fright.

The girls were at their grandparents' house on that magical spring night of swaying oaks and cloudbursts and the pitter-patter of rain on the eaves. The racket kept them rambunctious, and the soda pop they begged from their grandpa gave them the giggles rather than calming them down for bedtime stories. At Sang's house their mother was filled with the same excitement, because her sisters Roxanna and Etta Mae were expected any minute to join Sang and Maude for chicken dinner. Etta Mae, whose cooking was to die for, was bringing her coleslaw with green apples and pecans.

Aunt Maude and Uncle Joe had nine children. Aunt Maude wasn't much bigger than we were at twelve and thirteen, but she sure could work a lot harder than we could. Our visits to her house were spent sitting around in a big, high-ceilinged room, looking at all the old stuff in the room. Big old milk churns, sausage grinder, iron pots and pans for cornbread — old iron everything. They were all in a corner of the room. We just looked at them.

JULIA

Aunt Julia was born in 1887 and died in 1923, the fourth child of Grandpa Emanuel and Sophronia Dukes. She was married to Uncle T.B. Wilson.

In the first years of the 20th century, an era that came to be called the "American Century," a fine-looking young couple sauntered down Farish Street, in the Negro business section of Jackson between the Baptist church and the Methodist church, along clothing stores, doctors' offices, the pool hall, pawn shops, and barber shops. Their destination: the photographer's studio. There they would don their finery as never before, he in a black suit with a tuxedo shirt and bow tie, seated in a rattan chair with twenty wicker swirls crowning its high back, she standing beside him in white lace cascading over sheer gauze, its scalloped flounces falling from the nape of her neck to the floral-carpeted floor. Beside the pillar painted on the backdrop, they cast their gazes solemnly at the camera. T.B. Wilson, the groom, dropped his long jaw with forthright intent while his bride's full cheeks shone in the studio light. Julia Dukes' round face bore a quiet smile and tender eyes and placid lips.

The modest little house where they lived following their wedding told a lot about them in its books and papers, collected letters and issues of the *Progressive Farmer.* On the shelves, one found Shakespeare and Mark Twain alike. Julia taught school in Marion and Hinds counties, and T.B. was both teacher and principal. He also became a full-time father to their five children when Julia died in 1923. While the Dukes, the Exposés, and other country relatives came visiting with fruits from their trees and potatoes and greens from their fields, T.B. Wilson shouldered the responsibility of those children himself. Never did he waver from the dream he had shared with Julia: these children would become wise, brave, and strong. With a proper education, they would be the state's new electorate. The future was in their hands.

AUNT ROXIE: THE QUIET SEAMSTRESS

Roxie was no rival in the kitchen; her talent was simply for the piano. As the musician for Friendship Missionary Baptist Church, she enjoyed playing, and she was admired for her music at Gold Link Tabernacle and Bethsheba Chapter Seven as well. With her husband, Willis, she owned and operated a live bait farm with red worms, wigglers, catalpa, grub worms, and crickets for sale. (In fact, it led to no end of jokes about the soft-spoken Roxanna "baiting" Willy and vice versa.) She sewed beautiful coats and dresses as well as fine men's and women's suits of gray, blue, and black gabardine and some of pin-striped flannel. On one balmy night in 1938, Roxie wore a box-pleated skirt and fine-tailored white blouse she'd just finished to show off to her sisters.

Sometimes Uncle Willis would take us out to his bait farm and show us how to put the bait on the hook of the fishing line. I couldn't seem to bait the hook while keeping the worm alive, but of course, Uncle Willis said that was the best way to catch fish, while the bait was still moving a lot. Sometimes he would take us riding in his car when he delivered bait to his customers. He made up for Aunt Roxie's taciturn manner.

Aunt Roxie used to have a few women over to her house occasionally for sewing lessons. She was, I think, the best seamstress of all. She could make suits for women and men, and any kind of dress was easy for her. One time when I was visiting her in the kitchen, she asked me how Mama made her coleslaw with the pecans and apples in it. She was going to make some small tuna sandwiches for the sewing ladies and wanted to serve the coleslaw with it.

Aunt Roxie was quiet, and she usually didn't say much unless someone asked her something, but when we visited, Jimmy, Darlene, and I were full of questions, especially about the bait and the farm and the worms. We'd ask, "Aunt Roxie, do you bait your own hook?" or "Are you ever scared that Uncle Willy might put a worm under your pillow or something?" We'd laugh, and Aunt Roxie would say, "But your Uncle Willis would never do that, not even to scare you. No, he would not." We thought it was funny. The other reason we always enjoyed visiting Aunt Roxie and Uncle Willis was that we also got to visit some city friends. Every time we went to Aunt Roxie's, we also went to visit them.

ETTA MAE: MAMA

Etta Mae was forever the cook. Working in her vegetable garden, her barnyard, and her kitchen to feed between thirteen and thirty people daily (adding to her own family the cotton pickers during harvest time), she wore simple frocks. Come Sundays, she paraded into church in her stark navy blue suit and crisp, white blouse with a wide, starched collar, generally with her signature paper flower tucked in at the bosom. Any suit or coat she wore framed her full-featured face with a wildly textured collar, and many a passerby took notice. The same air of confidence emanated from her words, because Etta Mae Dukes never repeated herself when she expressed her wishes, nor did she raise her voice for effect. All she needed to do was look at you, and you did what she wanted you to do or held your peace.

Etta Mae would chuckle almost without opening her mouth. Whatever was uttered had to jump like a barrel of monkeys to get a belly laugh out of her, but this did sometimes happen. Embroidery, quilting, and canning were Mama's things.

AUNT GLADYS: THE MOVIE STAR

That night, the soft scent of cedar floated through the twilight with the streaming squeal of male cicadas, as if they were sending up their applause for the two sisters who waltzed up the porch of Sang's house in their pastel dresses, for on this outing when they were "off-duty"—no children, no husbands, no errands, no chores—only jubilation brought them together. From here on out, it was girl talk, and as the moon rose in the sky, their stories interrupted each other like the sheet lightning that flickered through the fields.

There is an old saying that goes, "If I tell you a hen dips snuff, all you gotta do is look under the wing." Well, that night (as usual), all the Dukes girls dipped snuff, Sang and Maude sinking back into their rocking chairs, Roxie and Etta Mae on the porch swing, each of them pulling it out of tiny tin boxes in their purses that looked like match boxes or pill boxes, but were, for all practical purposes, snuff boxes. They tucked the snuff inside their mouths between their lower lips and the gums of their teeth 'til their saliva melted it. On the swing, the two younger sisters spit the brown juice into a tin can they held between them. From their rocking chairs the two elders spit right over the porch into the grass, but the "hen" who really had something "under her wing" was the fifth sister, whose headlights now beamed up the gravel road from her long, white convertible that was as big as a boat.

In her soft, yellow dress with spaghetti straps and twirly skirt, the Movie Star had arrived. In fact, that's what they called her, since Gladys was the glamorous city girl from faraway Detroit, even if she was hardly a long-lost sister. Gladys turned up at any old time, as if she'd just come from the corner store. Her head swayed and bobbed with every word, and, just as her pretty lipstick lips never stopped smiling and chattering, her eyes never stopped darting up and down everything that fell within her gaze. Her hands flew as she talked, and she sank her body down in front of you, crossing her curvy legs and swinging her feet in open-toed pumps as if to prepare her pose for your pleasure.

She was also known as Marguerite, Lucretia, Jane, Ella, Elizabeth, and Carrie, for the simple reason that as a newborn, she drew names from everyone who stopped by, and her mother, Sophronia, kept them all. Gladys was married to Joe Newkirk, an insurance agent from Shreveport. Like the other Dukes girls, she hunted, fished, sewed, taught school, and played the piano. But this night, she had a lovely surprise for everyone: she also played the mandolin. It was this last item that sent her to the backseat of the car even before she strutted up the porch stairs: tucked under her arm was the most delicate piece of cherry-wood craftsmanship, its wide neck bearing twelve pegs strung with metal and gut, a kaleidoscope rose painted on parchment attached to its soundboard. Sometimes she played it as if that mandolin were a nightingale's nest on a Mediterranean shore, but tonight she pretended it was a ukulele and gave a swing to her tunes that moved the gals to cut up the living room floor. Gladys was a born performer, but the hooch she swigged from the femininely etched silver flask tucked in the inner pocket of her prim jacket gave an extra lilt to her tune.

If it goes without saying that the Dukes sisters, intelligent and refined as they were, commanded respect far and wide, it cannot be said enough how much they enjoyed each other on this particular night, kicking up their legs in a Charleston to the strings of Roxie's piano, swinging to the Victrola tunes that sailed out of its big horn filling the room with the notes of Ella, Billie, the Count, and the Duke. "How Long Has This Been Going On," the girls crooned, and they sank back and sighed through "I Thought About You," "There's a Lull in My Life," and "What Will I Tell My Heart." From "jungle music" to "A-Tisket A-Tasket" to Fats Waller on the jukebox, Gladys delivered a flair to match that of any Lindy hopper from the North. Her hair, swept up in waves and curls at the crown of her head, called attention to her hazel eyes and light complexion, not to mention her Coca-Cola bottle body, which made her the belle of the ball on social outings in her own neck of the woods, including the exclusive Pine Knob ski resort outside of Detroit, where she could be found draped in mink and sipping Cutty Sark from fine glasses.

At home with her sisters, another kind of acceptance gratified her. Here, she could share intimacies with Sang and Maude, Roxie and Etta Mae about those men who "made the world go 'round," the Diggs family in Detroit and the Marshalls of Maryland, for example. In her own city, Charles C. Diggs, Sr., a mortician, businessman, and community activist of Mississippi, had become the first black Democratic state senator and had authored the "Diggs Law" just a year earlier prohibiting racial or racially related discrimination in public places. This was the kind of power the Dukes girls fell for, and they saw it over and over in Thurgood Marshall. Hunting, fishing, mandolin and piano playing were Gladys's equipment.

Aunt Gladys came to live with Grandpa and Grandma during the last two years of their lives. She and Uncle Joe lived in Monroe, Louisiana, at that time, and had no children. Uncle Joe remained in Monroe-Shreveport and continued his work as an insurance agent. He took care of their family home. He came to Mississippi to be with Aunt Marguerite and to visit on the weekend. After the death of Grandma and Grandpa in 1936, Aunt Gladys and Uncle Joe moved to Detroit. To us, she looked like the women in the magazine, but she was Aunt Gladys.

The Brothers Dukes

Tobie: Preacher; Shug: Fisherman; Sonny: Professor

"Well, if Jesus didn't hear that stompin' yesterday, he lost his ears, is what I say!" Shug was commenting on Tobie's church service where he was a Holiness Faith minister. "He lost his nose, too," laughed Tobie, "if he couldn't smell that Sally Lou and her sweet savor. An' he lost his eyes if he couldn't see that pretty li'l netted hat o' hers fly right into her bosom once she took off gyratin' down the aisle!"

Yes, this was Tobie talking, the Reverend Gilbert Dukes, nephew of Gabriel and son of Emanuel Dukes, talking to his brother Shug about the distractions of the feminine turnout in the clapping and roving and swaying congregation. Such banter was bound to come up on their hunting trips when anything went flying by, even and especially, some choice words. Tobie and Shug lived but a couple hundred feet down the road from each other, so whenever Shug felt like wasting some tobacco or telling lies, he'd call a hunting party together. He'd let go of his gig for the day — the two-wheel, mule-drawn cart that he used to deliver the mail between Oloh and Columbia — wave good-bye to his wife, Mattie, top off his flask of whiskey, fill up his pouch with Prince Albert, and off he'd go to collect Tobie, his brother Sonny, and others.

None of them had the gun Shug had, a twelve-gauge automatic shotgun. Their guns had to be reloaded each time they shot it. Shug was serious — as serious about hunting as he was playful at lying. He'd tilt his head and roll his eyes as he spun his tales 'til there was no way he didn't convince you to be scared to death. Sonny, of course, was just the opposite. Known to his constituency as Professor Montes Dukes, there was no small talk falling from his sober lips. Direct, exact, and formal, Sonny had a reputation as a tyrant for strict discipline. Having graduated from Alcorn A & M College, he ran a tight ship at George Washington Carver Elementary School in Indianola, north of Jackson, where he served as principal. Furthermore, as a mortician, Sonny Dukes developed a chemical formula for embalming fluid that is still in use today.

Then again, Sonny was a "looker," both in terms of "lookin' good" and "lookin' *at.*" His wife, Lucille, and his daughter Mercedes were the first to notice, but he was mostly a listener. So when the three brothers were out together, it was Shug who did the talking. Now it could be that Sonny grew shy after delivering his speech that day at the podium before a large crowd and the top plate of his dentures fell out. Good thing he had a clean handkerchief with him so he could just dust them off and pop them back in like it was nobody's business, but who did he think he was kidding? Not a soul laughed, yet they all saw it. So

Montes (Sonny), Mama's brother, was still serious in the 1950s.

much for sobriety. Shug could usually count on Sonny to catch his humor.

That day in the forest, the gray-green that filtered the morning was like the veil of a lady's hat, enmeshed with moss on muscadine vines, frail as a net of mulberry threads. Ferns and foliage covered patches of still, black water. Berries and cones on hardwood trees surprised with the sounds of their fall. Ducks dipped their beaks in the lake with their tails in the air. Birds cooed. A live oak sang its history as Spanish moss moved like a beard in the breeze. Fragrant like dust, it spoke to the senses, such that not only

192

Mama and her remaining siblings during a visit in 1960.

somber Sonny, but also fun-loving, tell-tale Tobie, and even Shug, the Sugar-Man himself, fell to the spell of the forest.

Now, there are those who do believe what came to pass: the long-extinct ivory-billed woodpecker, whose notes were sad but clear as a clarinet, came to light its head against the bark to locate the source of hidden grubs. It bore its bill into the tree several feet deep down through its trunk, and there it found a boy-turned-man, born and dead too soon, who came of age to know, who knowing, sought to vote, who voting, lived no more. No lake and no sweetheart took the lad, but the black cherry tree shivered in the wind, and the crimson-crested wood-pecker made its nest in the hole it dug with its ivory bill, and it had no reason to sing its plaintive song.

Uncle Tobie lived in a big, white house down at the Friendship community, he and Aunt Jenny. He adopted Aunt Jenny's two children, twins Oliver and Olivia. Uncle Tobie's church was the noisiest church I had ever been in. Everybody was up on the floor and looked like they were dancing. He was in the pulpit and I didn't understand what he was saying. The singing drowned out his voice. The congregation seemed to be in a world of their own, like in a trance. He would clap his hands and everything came to order. When we visited Uncle Tobie, we sat around on the front porch and Aunt Jenny gave us cookies she made. Uncle Shug and Aunt Mattie lived just across the road from Uncle Tobie, and with all his fishing adventures he invented the flugger crippled-minnow fishing lure (wood and steel hooks), along with perfecting the art of rolling Prince Albert Tobacco into cigarettes and holding them on his bottom lip while talking. He was like an older brother to us instead of an uncle, telling jokes that kept us laughing.

Uncle Sonny and Aunt Lucile never failed to fill up the trunk of his big, black car with potatoes and vegetables from Mama's garden. We looked forward to their visits during the summer months. He and Mama would laugh and talk and we didn't know what it was about. His godchild, Dr. Hull in Los Angeles, and attorney Charles Lloyd were students of his. They remember how he kept the students in line and ran the school like a military man. The students were given a chance to succeed.

Grandpa Dukes' Adventures

Late in the afternoon one summer, my cousin Geraldine ("Little Bit") and I sat down and talked. We talked about all the Dukes that had died and the Exposés and Watts. It was sad when we realized not too many older ones were left. My older brother Luther ("Tootsie"), who died February 10, 2010, told me many stories about all the Dukes he remembered and the Exposés, but Cousin Geraldine ("Little Bit") had some funny stories to tell of their adventures. Little Bit remembers going down to Grandpa's by horse and buggy. Their buggy had a front and back seat like a car. She and her brother would sit on the back seat with their legs hanging down. It was less than ten miles, but it seemed like they were going across country. Crossing a bridge over a small stream, they'd jump off and see who could outrun the buggy to Grandpa's house. Years later, Uncle Sonny had a home built for Grandpa and Grandma near town, with electricity and a fish pond out back, very near Uncle Shug and Aunt Mattie's across a brook.

The visits were on Friday or Saturday night because they stayed overnight. All the sisters and brothers and children brought their children. Many of the young children slept on pallets on the floor. The mothers would be in the kitchen cooking dinner — vegetables, chicken and dumplings, egg pies, tea cakes, and a lot of lemonade. All the Dukes fished, so there were a lot of fish. Cousin Alphonso was taught by Grandpa to shoot a gun, catch catfish, and rope horses. The older ones killed so many quail, turkey, and squirrels that the wagon had to bring the load home. It took half the night to clean and dress all they killed. The feast was on.

One time, some men came out to Grandpa's with mineral rods to search for gold. Grandpa had buried gold pieces on his property and in logs. The men tested their equipment, but the gold was found by a family member and each child got a gold piece. It's been handed down through the generations. Little Bit and her brother were big helpers to Grandpa and Grandma. Grandpa got up early every day, got dressed in a white shirt, necktie, pants, and Stacy Adams shoes. After breakfast, they took him for a walk — one on each side, the way Tootsie and Boy Noah did when they visited as young boys.

One day, after they got up for breakfast, Grandma didn't have any flour to make biscuits. She cooked some corn bread instead. Little Bit and her brother started laughing and took off over to Uncle Shug's. They ran all the way — only a short skip and a jump. Uncle Shug and Aunt Mattie would certainly have some biscuits for breakfast. No sooner had they got there than Grandma was right behind them to take them back to the house. They told Aunt Mattie they never had corn bread for breakfast and continued laughing.

Little Bit and sisters Eula Bell and Vera were trying to see how they could get some grapes from the vines that were way up a tree and out on a limb. The vines were halfway between Grandpa's and Uncle Shug's house. Finally, they decided to have Little Bit be the lookout on the ground while Eula Bell and Vera climbed the tree. If anyone came, like Grandma, Little Bit would whistle and they'd climb down. Well, just as they got up the tree and out on the limb with a few grapes, Grandma came walking up and Little Bit started whistling and whistling. She told Little Bit that girls don't whistle. About that time, Eula Bell and Vera saw Grandma and fell out of the tree. They hit the ground running. Grandma looked up and saw the grape vines hanging and grapes all over the ground when they fell.

Aunt Mattie and Uncle Shug were going downtown one day, and Little Bit and her brother asked Grandpa if they could go to buy a Baby Ruth candy bar. Grandpa gave her brother two nickels and Little Bit one dime. She fell out crying because the dime was smaller. He took her by the hand and explained that the dime was smaller, but had the same value as the two nickels. Little Bit finally stopped crying. All the grandchildren would continue to visit regularly, spend the night, and help out. They loved their Grandpa.

Epilogue: Full Circle

One day I was sitting in the nurse's lounge in the intensive care unit of the Los Angeles hospital where I worked and flipping through a magazine. I came across a picture of little children sitting on bales of hay in the back of a pickup truck. They were riding through the countryside on a gravel road, on their way to a picnic. A flood of memories swept through my head, all about my childhood. Papa's old pickup truck or old Emma that pulled the wagon full of cotton, or hay that was piled on top for our daily ride of adventure.

It was a time in our history that has passed, one that too many never knew about or understood. So, this story needs to be told. It is another perspective of southern Negro farm families, of people who farmed their own land — grandparents, great-grandparents, aunts and uncles — generations of farmers who left their mark. The older ones are dead now and what's left of them, besides our memories, is the next generation — mine and beyond. Our memories keep them alive, in spite of new ways of living today and the fact that many who will read these words have never felt the soil of Mississippi under their bare feet.

It seems so long ago that we were all together as children, so many brothers and sisters, with Mama and Papa looking on. My parents and nine siblings have passed on and are now memories I keep in my heart. Of the last four of us, Carzella, who lives up the road from the farmhouse, and Paul, who lives in downtown Columbia, never left Missis-

The family of Noah and Etta Mae Exposé in 1942. This is the only existing photograph of the entire family.

sippi. Darlene moved to Hattiesburg after many years in Washington, D.C. As for me, I have moved back to the farmhouse where we all grew up.

Coming home has been bittersweet, because it is a different way of life here now. The cotton and corn fields have been replaced by hay fields, with cows grazing all along the open countryside. Long stretches of nothing but tall trees line both sides of the road, scenic during the day and pitch black at night, an occasional deer appearing out of nowhere to dart like lightning across the empty spaces. The little old gravel roads are paved now, and house trailers dot the landscape. Can you imagine a garbage truck picking up the garbage once a week out in front of the house? Papa wouldn't have believed it!

Occasionally an old tractor or a rusty old pickup truck can be seen under a shed as I pass a house remembered from long ago. Not only do all the roads have names now, many of them commemorate the old people who are gone, and mailboxes carry house numbers on them. There are security lights in all the yards and the lawns are sculptured, with SUVs parked on concrete driveways. All the country schools relocated years ago to nearby towns, leaving only the churches to continue as the community force that binds the people together.

It's easier to fly closer to home now, with the small airport in Hattiesburg, about twenty-five miles east, and a newer one sixty-five miles south in Gulfport-Biloxi. For years, the Jackson, Mississippi airport was the closest one, one hundred miles to the north. Small shopping malls have been built out of downtown Hattiesburg, on Highway 98, with places to spend money all along the highway. Our town, Columbia, has two small shopping areas along Highway 98, twelve miles west, for us country folks to shop at as well. Banks, service stations, and eateries line the highway now.

The only structure in our yard is our house. The big A-frame barn burned years ago, in the 1970s. Papa sold the windmill. Our water supply, the well, water pump and the windmill water have been replaced by the central county water line. The tin-enclosed carport was torn down years ago, as was the old block smokehouse behind the house. Lightning struck one of the big oak trees in front of the house and it had to be cut down. The one still standing is on its way out also. Soon it too, like the crop duster man who used to fly over it to terrify and delight us, will be a lovely memory.

A few schoolmates continue to live in the community and nearby towns, as well as some who moved away for years and have, like I have, returned to their roots. Among them are the daughters of Albert Jackson and K.C. Lumzy and a couple of John Watts' sons (the John Watts who made all the syrup at his sugarcane mill). We have all renewed our friendships and walk down the many memory lanes of our childhood together.

The grandson, Jimmy, of our white neighbor, old man Walter Harris, lives just down the road. Up the road are our old friends Shirley Rose and her brother, Horace Melvin, and his wife, Mae; their sister Charree lives out near Hattiesburg. Vera and Barry (Walter Harris's son) have passed on, as have Joyclyn and Carol, but their brother Royce maintains Vera and Barry's old house.

My new white neighbors live within walking distance, three to five city blocks away. Through them I have renewed my country living habits, feeding their dogs, cats, ducks and horses. I watch their four-wheelers get stuck in the mud of one of their ponds and am secure in the knowledge that the reliable tractor will pull them out. They invite me to bonfires in the middle of the wintry woods, and I am kept busy stacking the firewood they deliver to my backyard.

Jimmy will see a big tree limb broken from the pecan tree in the back yard and just drive his tractor across the yard and drag it to the edge of the woods. His cows mooing at nighttime in a nearby pasture keep me reminded that I am back in the country. My move back to Mississippi has been a good thing.

Home again is home forever.

Index

Index

Milton Keynes UK
Ingram Content Group UK Ltd.
UKHW041830121124
451104UK00012B/97